H. Herbert Pain

Englishmen, Israelites, Turks, Edomites, Politics and Prophecy

H. Herbert Pain

Englishmen, Israelites, Turks, Edomites, Politics and Prophecy

ISBN/EAN: 9783337088590

Printed in Europe, USA, Canada, Australia, Japan

Cover: Foto ©Lupo / pixelio.de

More available books at **www.hansebooks.com**

Gen. 49. 10.

Micah 5. 8.   Deut. 33. 17.

ENGLISHMEN ISRAELITES.

TURKS EDOMITES.

POLITICS and PROPHECY.

A Revised and Enlarged Reprint from
"The Covenant People," with Colored Map.

H. HERBERT PAIN.

A Founder & Member of the Council of the British Israel Association.

(*Metropolitan, Provincial & Colonial.*)

SECOND EDITION: TENTH THOUSAND.

LONDON:
Robt. Banks & Son, Racquet Court, Fleet Street.

ENTERED AT STATIONERS' HALL.

S. BUSH & SON,
PRINTERS,
42, High Street, Bromley, Kent.

PREFACE.

HOW is it that the British Empire, the greatest Empire the world has ever seen, has attained and bids fair to maintain its present splendid position? May it not be accounted for by the supposition that it is identical with the Stone Kingdom of Daniel, and the House of Israel of the Old Testament Prophets?

We live in times of great disquietude, so far as the European political situation is concerned, and no one can tell from day to day, if the dreaded Eastern Question may not call for solution at any moment. All the Great Powers of Europe are armed to the teeth, in anticipation of the dismemberment of the Ottoman Empire and the consequent struggle for " the sick man's inheritance."

If the British Nation, with America, be identical with the House of Joseph, as is the contention of the following argument, then the destruction of Turkey will be brought about by their joint intervention. What the ultimate cause may be, that will call for our interference in the affairs of the Sultan's dominions, can only be foreseen by a close study of the political intelligence of our well-informed Daily Press, in the light of the literal interpretation of prophecy.

The declaration of the Prophet Isaiah is pregnant with meaning at the present time:

"One calleth unto me out of Seir, Watchman, what of the night? Watchman, what of the night?

The watchman said "The morning cometh, and also the night: if ye will enquire, enquire ye: come ye again."

Meanwhile, it is the object of this Pamphlet to draw the attention of the public to the more sure words of prophecy; "whereunto ye do well to take heed as unto a light that shineth in a dark place," that they may not be unprepared for the anxious times that are so near at hand, and thus better realise the special promise of divine protection to our Nation, as declared by the Prophet Isaiah.

In order that the reader may not be wearied in following this subject, the arguments have been stated as concisely as possible, and the texts on which the statements are based, have been quoted as well as the references, so as to save those who may not have the time or the inclination, the tedium of turning them up.

A Map of the Promised Land, on a reduced scale from the original; drawn to the special design of the Writer by Stanford, is added, so that it may bring home to the mind of the reader more forcibly than words or argument can do; how wonderfully the Nation is unconciously fulfilling its destiny, by the occupation of Egypt, and in undertaking the present Expedition into the Soudan, &c.

If the views hereafter stated, are expressed in a somewhat homely manner, it is hoped that that may not detract from the interest which it is sincerely trusted will be aroused in the subject matter; but on the contrary induce a further study of the Works recommended on the closing pages of this Pamphlet, and the acceptance of this great truth, that the Lost House of Israel is found in the British Nation.

H. HERBERT PAIN.

September, 1896.

PREFACE TO THE SECOND EDITION.

IT is naturally a source of gratification to the Writer to announce, that within a few months of the publication of this work, it has been found necessary to issue a second edition of five thousand copies, as the result of its favourable reception by the public.

The opportunity thus afforded, has been taken advantage of to correct typographical errors in the first edition; also to strengthen one or two passages in the text, and to insert a few additional foot-notes.

Some slight additions also have been made to the colouring of the Map; and an Appendix is added, containing information which it is hoped will be found interesting.

The Writer particularly wishes it to be understood, that in endeavouring to arrange the sequence of events in the second portion of this Pamphlet, he has no desire to lay down too definite a theory as to the order, or details, of the fulfilment of events foretold by the Old Testament Prophets. That time alone will declare.

Obviously however "the hand-writing on the wall" of the Prophetical Scriptures is more easy to interpret as the time draws nearer for its realisation, and especially is this the case to those who are able to study them by the light of British-Israel Truth.

Meantime we shall all do well to take heed to our Saviour's command—WATCH !

H. HERBERT PAIN.

Bromley, Kent.
    March, 1897.

ENGLISHMEN ISRAELITES.

ANGLO-ISRAELISM, or the Identity of the British people with the lost House of Israel, as distinguished from the Jews, or the House of Judah, is a question not of doctrine but interpretation. It is therefore a subject on which men of all shades of religious opinion may meet on the common ground of belief in the Bible.

Certain promises and blessings were made to Abraham, Isaac, and Jacob—or Israel—which were to be fulfilled to their descendants, the Twelve Tribes of Israel, in the latter days (Gen. 49. 1). By common consent the expression "latter days" is held to mean this—the Christian—Dispensation.

The Early History of the Children of Israel is too well known to need repetition. For the purpose of explaining this theory, we may pass on to the division of the twelve-tribed nation under Rehoboam into two kingdoms: namely, the House of Judah, over whom Rehoboam reigned as King in Jerusalem, which consisted of the Tribes of Judah, Levi, and Benjamin; and the House of Israel, reigned over by Jeroboam at Samaria.* The latter called "the kingdom, even ten tribes;" (1 Kings 11. 35), was composed of Reuben, Simeon, Dan, Napthali, Gad, Asher, Issachar, Zebulon, Ephraim and Manasseh. Benjamin, although one of the tribes of the House of Israel—not Judah—

*Or Shechem—1 Kings 12. 25.

was in accordance with the words of the prophet Ahijah, lent to David's reigning representative, "that David my servant may have a lamp alway before me in Jerusalem."

The Tribes of Judah and Levi went into captivity to Babylon accompanied by the Tribe of Benjamin who was part of and was called "all Israel," though incorporated for the time being with Judah, known, commonly speaking, as the Jews.

Ezra and Nehemiah, in recording the names and families of those who returned from Babylon, speak of Benjamin as "all Israel," and it is in this sense, and not as referring to the Ten Tribes of the House of Israel wholly, that this expression is to be understood. That this contention is correct will be readily seen on referring to the context.

Although Benjamin remained with Judah in Palestine until after our blessed Lord's crucifixion and the commencement of the Roman siege of Jerusalem in A.D. 70, it can be inferentially proved that Benjamin did not share with Judah the punishment which followed on the Roman siege and dispersion.

In support of this argument, the following passages are submitted:

Jer. 6. 1, "Flee for safety, ye children of Benjamin, out of Jerusalem, . . . for evil looketh forth from the north and a great destruction." *

---

* All the Scriptural quotations in this Pamphlet are taken from the Revised Version of the Bible, unless otherwise stated.

Matt. 24. 15—17, "When therefore ye see the abomination of desolation, which was spoken of by Daniel the prophet standing in the holy place, (let him that readeth understand), then let them that are in Judæa flee unto the mountains : " [*i.e.*, of Beth-haccherem. Jer. 6. 1.]

These prophetic warnings, given in anticipation of the siege and destruction of Jerusalem, it is believed the Benjaminites took heed to, as Eusebius, in his *Historia Ecclesiæ*, makes mention of some Christian "Jews" having escaped unhurt before the siege. The quotation is as follows :— "The people of the Church in Jerusalem were directed, by a solemn warning given in a revelation to approved men among them, to remove from the city before the war commenced, and to take for their dwelling-place a city of Perea, by name Pella ; wherein, accordingly, they who believed on Christ abode, after quitting Jerusalem" (Book 3, 5. 2). The opportunity probably occurred at the time when the Roman General, for some inexplicable reason, temporarily raised the siege, thus enabling these Christian Benjaminite "Jews" to escape the horrors that ensued on the renewal of the same.

Zechariah (13. 6—9) has a significant reference to this event :

"Smite the shepherd, and the sheep shall be scattered ; and I will turn mine hand upon the little ones.

"And it shall come to pass, that in all the land, saith the Lord, two parts (Judah and Levi) therein shall be cut off and die ; but the third shall be left therein,

"And I will bring the third part (Benjamin) through the fire, and . . . they shall call on my name, and I will hear them: I will say, It is my people; and they shall say the Lord is my God."

The same Prophet further predicts the severance of Benjamin from Judah, in Chapter 11. 7—14;

"So I fed the flock of slaughter, verily the poor of the flock. And I took unto me two staves; the one I called Beauty [Mosaic Covenant] and the other I called Bands [the "Binders" of Judah and Benjamin]; and I fed the flock.

"And I cut off the three shepherds in one month; [priests, judges, and lawyers, *vide* Pusey], for my soul was weary of them, and their soul also loathed me.

"And I took my staff Beauty, and cut it asunder, that I might break my covenant [the Mosaic] which I had made with all the peoples.

"And it was broken in that day: *and thus the poor of the flock that gave heed unto me knew that it was the word of the Lord.*

"Then I cut asunder mine other staff, even Bands, that I might break the brotherhood between Judah and Israel."

To return to

The Northern Kingdom of the House of Israel
under Jeroboam. It was eventually carried captive from Samaria to Assyria, in B.C. 740, by Tiglath Pileser, and by Shalmanesar in B.C. 721.

From that time the *history* of the House of Israel ceases in Scripture.

Prophecy declares that they shall be found in the Isles of the Sea, North-West from Palestine; *vide* the following passages, which refer exclusively to the ten-tribed House of Israel, as is evident by the contexts, *e.g.*

Jeremiah 3. 12, "Go, and proclaim these words towards the *North* [*i.e.*, from Palestine], and say, Return, thou backsliding Israel" (in contrast to her "treacherous" sister Judah, *vide* ver. 7).

Chap. 23. 8, ". . . . the House of Israel out of the *North* country."

Chap. 31. 8, "O Lord, save thy people the remnant of Israel . . . from the *North* country."

Isaiah 49. 12, "Lo, these shall come from far: and lo, these from the *North* and from the *West*: and these from the land of Sinim," or as it is rendered in the Vulgate, *Terra Australis*, the land of Australia: now known to us as "the Bush Country," which is almost the exact rendering of the original word, *Sinim*, "the land of bushes."

Chap. 11. 11, "The Lord shall set His face again the *second time* to recover the remnant of his people . . . from . . . Egypt [now practically in our possession] . . . and from the *Islands of the Sea*."

Chap. 24. 15, "Wherefore glorify the Lord in the East [India], even the name of the Lord God of Israel in the *Isles of the Sea* [or West]."*

* The Rev. F. R. A. Glover, in his work *England the Remnant of Judah*, on page 123, quotes the remark of a friendly Rabbi to the effect that the Hebrew phrase איים here rendered Isles of the Sea, is regularly employed by the Jews of to-day in describing the British Isles.

The Hebrew ים the Sea, means also the *West*.

Chap. 42. 10, " Sing unto the Lord a new (the Christian) song, and his praise from the *end* of the earth; ye that go down to the *sea*, and all that is therein, the *Isles*, and the inhabitants thereof."

Chap. 49. 1, " Listen, O *Isles*, unto me: and hearken ye people from *far*."

Jeremiah 31. 9—11, " For I am a father to Israel, and Ephraim is my first-born. Hear the word of the Lord, O ye nations, and declare it in the *Isles afar off*, and say: He that scattered Israel will gather him, and keep him as a shepherd doth his flock."

In the light of history and present events, these texts undoubtedly point to the British Isles, as no other Islands in any part of the World, either in the past or present, have contained a people who from their national career answer to the above description and localisation North-West of Palestine. Those who are inclined to let their independent judgment be biased by the writings of Commentators, should remember that those exponents of the Scriptures, in many instances, had not the advantage of basing their interpretations on the rapid development and fulfilment of prophecy to such an extent as we possess in the present century.

Now to trace the House of Israel,

From Assyria to the British Isles.

(Condensed from " British-Israel Truth," chap. vii. by "Oxonian." with sundry other extracts from "Israel's Wanderings," by the same author.)

" The scene of the captivity was the modern province of Azerbijan, with the adjoining south-western shore-line of the Caspian Sea. The names of to-day † are identical with those mentioned in 2

† See coloured Map at end of Pamphlet.

Kings 17. 6, etc. Thus Haru=*Hara*, Abhar=*Habor*, Ala-mut=*Halah* (LXX *Ala-e*); while Ouzan of to-day is the Gozen of the tenth century A.D., and the *Gozan* of the ancients. This River Gozan on the south, the River Araxes (now called Aras), which according to Herodotus flowed "*towards the rising sun*" on the north, the Caspian Sea on the east, with the Tigris and Euphrates on the West, formed the boundaries of their new but temporary home."

The account of their removal from this place is thus stated by Esdras (Book 2. chap. 13. 40—46):

"These are the ten tribes which were carried away prisoners out of their own land in the time of Osea the king, whom Shalmanasar the King of Assyria led away captive, and he carried them over the waters and so came they into another land.

" But they took this counsel among themselves, that they would leave the multitude of the heathen, and go forth into a further country, where never mankind dwelt,

"That they might there keep their statutes, which they never kept in their own land.

" And they entered into Euphrates by the narrow passages of the river.

" For the most High then showed signs for them, and held still the flood, till they were passed over.

" For through that country there was a great way to go, namely, of a year and a half: and the same region is called Arsareth.

"Then dwelt they there until the latter time."

To resume our summary of the argument presented in chap. vii. of *British Israel Truth*.

Ar-sareth is identified with the City of Sereth, on the River Sereth, a tributary stream of the Danube near Odessa. *Ar* is the Greek transliteration of two Hebrew words meaning severally "Hill" or "City"; and *Sareth* is of course identical with *Sereth*.

The account given by Esdras of the migration of the Ten Tribes is identical with the account given by Herodotus of the migration of the great Scythian nation from Asia into Europe. Herodotus says that the Scythians crossed the Araxes and came to the land of the Kimmerians* on the north-west of the Black Sea. This was about the year B.C. 650. The Median revolution against the supremacy of Assyria was definitely successful shortly before the year 650 B.C., an opportunity which Israel doubtless seized to escape in the manner described by Esdras. There ought to be no difficulty, therefore, in connecting the Scythians and the Israelites, as *their migration was identical in its starting-point, destination, and date!*

* "Who were the Kimmerians, whom the Scuths found dwelling in the country of Arsereth? *They also were Israelites.* They bear one of the names of outcast Israel, viz., the name of *Khumri*.

How they came there I know not. But they could not well have been in the captivity, for Ezra's account deals with those Israelites who escaped into Europe from Media. They must therefore, have escaped from the land of Israel during the period of Assyrian invasion. Is there any evidence of this? I know of none except this, which I take from a pamphlet of Colonel Gawler, entitled "Our Scythian Ancestors Identified with Israel." In this the author refers to a book written by a Jew, the Rev. M. Sailman, in 1818, entitled, "Researches in the East; an Important Account of the Ten Tribes." Mr. Sailman states (pp. 20, 21), that *many of the people did not go into captivity, but evaded the calamity*, going off with their flocks, and turning *Nomads*, and that the chief or prince, whom they appointed could muster 120,000 horse and 100,000 foot." Such a fact as this would amply satisfy the question of the Kimmerians. "*Israel's Wanderings*" (p. 56).

The Ten Tribes thus escaped about eighty years after their deportation from Samaria—" For a small moment have I forsaken thee " (Isa. liv. 7)—and have been found in Europe in the middle of the seventh century as the Scüths of Herodotus.

It is remarkable that the Upper Euphrates, is known as *Murad-Su*, a name which looks suspiciously like the Hebrew *Morad*, " descent." While close to the pass in the mountain chain separating Erzerum from Kars, a river rises and flows down northwards to the Black Sea; its name, in its upper course, is in one map given as *Israel*-su—Israel river. Has this no significance?

Colonel Gawler, in "*Our Scythian Ancestors*," quotes the following from transactions of the Biblical Archæological Society (Vol. iii. Part 1): " The Old Gravestones in the Crimea " writes Neubauer, " which are now recognised as genuine by all men of learning, attest that there were Jewish (*sic*) communities in the Crimea as early as the year A.D. 6, and that the Jews there *held themselves to be descended from the ten tribes*." The inscriptions are as follows:

"This is the tombstone of Buki, the son of Izchak, the priest. May his rest be in Eden at the time of the salvation of Israel. In the year 702 of the years of our exile (=A.D. 6)."

" Rabbi Moses Levi died in the year 726 of our exile (=A.D. 30)."

"Zadok the Levite, son of Moses, died 4000 after the creation, 785 of our exile (=A.D., 89)."

These inscriptions evidently could not refer to the Jews, who at that time were still in Palestine; they must therefore refer to the House of Israel.

Herodotus is careful to distinguish between the Scythian nation and the tribes living among them having Scythian habits, but who where not Scythians by tradition or language. The "*wandering*" Scüths who were settled in Arsereth claimed that their national existence had only lasted 1000 years to the day when Darius invaded them. That was about the year B.C. 500. Then they were first a nation about 1500—*the very epoch of the exodus* under Moses: while the tradition that Tar-gitaus,[*] their leader was the son of a god and of the daughter of one of the Scüthic rivers, may point to the familiar story of Moses in the bulrushes of the rivers of Egypt.

Those who lived nearest to Greece—the Getæ—believed, Herodotus tells us, in their *immortality*, and that there is *no other God but their own*. They think that they do not really die, but that when they departed this life they go to *Zal-Moxis*: they were the noblest and most just of all the peoples occupying the Thracian peninsula.[†] It has been pointed out by the late Colonel Gawler, that this name is possibly a Greek corruption of *Moses*, with the prefix *Sar*, "lord."

It is also a striking evidence that a town on the south bank of the Danube, near its mouth, bears the name *Isak-cha* to the present day.

Herodotus further mentions the Tribes into which the Scüthic nation was divided—the Royal Tribe and five others; the former being the

---

[*] This name may contain the same form as Getal, Sagetai.
[†] Herodotus iv. 93. They are naturally confused with the Thracians, as living on the Thracian side of the Danube. At a later period they will be found occupying Roumania on the north of that river.

"largest and bravest, and looking down upon all the other tribes in the light of slaves." In this there is something of the spirit of Ephraim; but the Royal Tribe may have included other Tribes of Israel. Prof. Rawlinson thinks that there may have been at all times Three great tribes among the Royal Scüths. On this supposition there were *Eight Tribes of Scüths.* Now (Dan and Simeon having escaped)* Eight Tribes of Israelites had been originally carried captive.

It is remarkable that Sharon Turner says, "*Eight* Anglo-Saxon governments were established in the Island. This state of Britain has been improperly denominated the Saxon Heptarchy. When all the kingdoms were settled, they formed an Octarchy."

Subsequent to the time of Herodotus, there are but scanty allusions to Scüthia and the Scüths. The few facts seem to be briefly these. About B.C. 438, the Scüths extended their dominion to the eastern side of the Kimmerian Bosphorus, or the Straits of Yeni-kaleh. This territory they continued to hold till 304. During the reign of Philip of Macedon, or about 350 B.C., the Getae, noticed previously as the southern vanguard of Scüthic Israel, retired to the north of the Danube, where they are found later, under the name of Dacians, occupying the Danubian Principalities,

---

* According to the Author of "*Israel's Wanderings,*" Simeon escaped from the captivity, but did not, as a body, share in the migrations of Dan into Ireland. Oxonian under the title of "Kymric Israel among the Gentiles," devotes a chapter in tracing Simeon *back* from west to east, through South Europe till they find a resting place in Galatia. Thence in company with Benjamin, as explained later on, they pass into Central Europe.

and the neighbouring portion of Hungary. Strabo has pointed out what Posidonius has related, "*and they even abstain from animal food from religious motives.*" About 250 B.C., there was an immigration into Scuthia of some "Kelts" from Galatia, who became absorbed amongst the main mass of the Scuthic nation.

Finally we have a notice of the Scuths as still occupying part of the Scuthia of Herodotus, about the year 115 B.C., in connection with the early aggressive movements of Mithridates of Pontus.

Some of the Scythian customs are plainly of a Hebrew origin. They made booths, like the Israelites. In offering sacrifices, they placed the bones of the animals beneath the cauldron, set them alight, and so boiled the meat. Professor Rawlinson connects this custom with the Israelitish usage described in Ezek. 24. 5 (A.V.), "Take the choice of the flock, and burn also the bones under it, and make it boil well." Herodotus further adds (4, 63) that they *never used swine* (the unclean animal of the Hebrews) in their sacrifices.

The record of their achievements in war goes far to confirm this association of the Scythians with the vanished tribes of Israel. The prophet Micah (5, 8) anticipates that: "The remnant of Jacob should be *among the nations*, in the midst of many peoples, *as a lion* . . . who, *if he go through, treadeth down and teareth in pieces, and there is none to deliver.*" In the year B.C. 628, the Scythian armies invaded Media from their recently-won settlements in Europe, and defeating the Medes, became masters of Asia. The rising power of Babylon was for twenty-eight years subservient to them. So, too, in B.C. 508 (Herodotus Bk. 4), when the Persian Emperor, Darius, invaded their European country, his final conflict with the Scythians was disastrous for the armies of Persia. Similarly, the southern Scythians, known at various times as Getæ, or Dacians, repulsed the haughty aggression of Greece and Rome: so that there was not one of the four great heathen Empires but experienced the prowess of this nomad nation. *This was foretold of Israel.*

The name "Scyth" (pronounced Skyth) recalls the "Scoth," or "Booths," which symbolised the *wandering* life of *Israel*. The Scythian nation therefore, settled at first circ. B.C. 650, on the banks of the Dniester and the Sereth, down to the shores of the Black Sea adjoining, and by the date at which Herodotus compiled his history (B.C. 450) had extended their dominion a considerable distance inland to the north. In Bk. 4, 101, he tells us that their territory occupied, roughly, a square of 4000 furlongs each way, with a base on the Black Sea between the Danube and the Don. That distance is just 500 miles—the identical distance indicated by Herodotus. Measure at right angles to this base, from the Don end, and the right side of the square brings you to Moscow. On the left hand to the border of Poland. The Don coincides with the greater part of the line on the right, while the Carpathian range of mountains answers to that on the left. The direction of the Scythian square, therefore, was south-east and north-west.

The marshes in which rise the Dnieper originate also the Duna, the Niemen, and the Vistula (some at least of its main feeders), which flow directly into the harbours of the Baltic, distant only some 200 miles. The Vistula further communicates by continuous waterways, across the central plain of Germany, with the valleys of the Oder and the Elbe. Thus the way lay open for the Scythian nation to cross the Baltic, or penetrate the level stretches of Upper Germany into Saxony and Scandinavia.

The English name and language were brought into Britain from the regions of the Elbe and the Danish Straits. From the opposite shore-lands of the German Ocean; Anglo-Saxon, Jute, Dane, and Norman migrated as swarms from a common hive.

So the chain stands complete. *Link the first*, from Samaria to the river Gozan. *Link the second*, from the Araxes to the Sereth. *Link the third*, from the Dnieper to the Elbe and the Danish Straits. *Link the fourth*, across the German Ocean into Britain.

Dan.

The history of this tribe is a peculiar one, and for reasons which will be seen hereafter, it is necessary to give some particulars of its early career.

So far back as B.C. 1285 the Danites were reproached by Deborah for remaining on board their ships on the occasion of the invasion of Israel by Sisera, captain of the host of Jabin, King of Canaan (Judges 5, 17). It is, therefore, highly improbable that the Danites would quietly remain to be deported to Assyria when they could escape by sea to the place which, in later times, was to give a home to their brethren who were carried captive to Assyria. Certain it is that the tribe of Dan entirely disappeared from Palestine.

Several writers believe that Dan became as good as extinct, but we know from Ezek. 48 that in the final division of the land Dan comes in for his share at the head of the list.

In Ezek. 27, 17—19 (A.V.), it says: "Dan also Javan going to and fro occupied in thy fairs:" The late Colonel Gawler, in his *Dan, the Pioneer of Israel*, states: "Now in three places in Daniel, where Alexander the Great is distinctly indicated, and one in Zechariah, Javan is translated 'Greece.'" Continuing, Col. Gawler says: "Josephus also (1, 6) mentions Javan as Greece. Hence Dan is indicated as in company with Greece trading with Tyre. English, Grecian, Irish, and Scandinavian histories teem with notices of a certain race called Danai, or Dannans, or Dannonii, who are either called Phœnicians or mentioned in company with Phœnicians; and almost wherever Phœnicians are said to have traded, *there* we hear either of these Danai, or we find a river or district named after Dan, according to the early custom of that tribe in the Scriptures (Judges 18. 29)."

Again, in the *Manual of Ancient History* (p. 214) is the following:—"From the middle of the sixteenth to the middle of the fourteenth century B.C., several colonies from Egypt, Phœnicia, and Phrygia settled in different parts of Greece. . . . . . The Phœnicians were, at that period, the undisputed masters of the Ægean."

Strabo (8, 5, 6) says: "Homer calls the whole

of Greece Argos, for he calls all Argives, as he calls them Danai and Achæi."

"I think," says Latham in his *Ethnology of Europe* (p. 157), "that the eponymus of the Argive Danai was no other than that of the Israelite tribe of Dan. . . . What a light would be thrown on the origin of the name Peloponnesus, and the history of the Pelopid family, if a *bona fide* nation of Pelopes, with unequivocal affinities and contemporary annals, had existed on the coast of Asia. Who would have hesitated to connect the two? *Yet with the Danai and the tribe of Dan this is the case, and no one connects them!*"

Quoting anew the late Colonel Gawler, in his excellent little work before referred to; on p. 16, he says: "Herodotus (4, 147) calls Theras, Regent of Lacedæmon, a Cadmæan and Phœnician. But with this confused assignment of Egyptian and Phœnician origin, which admirably suits the Israelites, we have this fact prominent: that a people called Danai arrived in Argos and extended their rule to all Greece, and that the Lacedæmonians, whether as Argives or Heraclidæ, were the most notable branch from this place."

"Again we will try to identify these Grecian Danai by their symbols. The serpent is held by various Hebrew and Chaldee writers to have been the cognizance of Dan" (Gen. 49, 17). "Ancient learned Jewish authorities unanimously assert that Dan bore Scorpio under an eagle" (Mazzaroth 39). "Ancient Hebrew and Chaldee authorities say that Dan bore on his standard a crowned serpent or basilisk held in the claws of an eagle" (Mazzaroth 41).

Also on page 17 of the same work, "the eagle is sometimes represented as holding the fulmen, or thunderbolt, in its claws. This might have been corrupted by the Greeks, who regarded the eagle as the minister of Jupiter, from Dan's eagle holding the serpent."

"The Emblem of St. John, one of the four evangelists, is the eagle. His mission was chiefly, if not entirely, among the Greeks.

"The *Vetus Chronicon Holsatiæ* asserts "the Danes and Jutse are Jews (*sic*) of the tribe of Dan."

"Dan's name is imprinted on the *Dan*ube, *Dan*-astris (now Dniester), *Dan*-apris (now Dnieper), and the *Don*.

"From the *Dan*-astris (Dniester) we follow it to its source, where we pick up the Vistula, at the mouth of which is *Dan*-zig on the shores of the Co-*dan* Gulf (now the Baltic), across to *Dan*nemora, opposite the Gulf of Finland, down the Baltic to *Dan*nemark, across the North Sea to the Humber, where we find the river *Don*, and go south, *Don*caster. Then we may cross to that undisputed head-quarters of *Dannans*,, the North of Ireland, anciently called Scotia, where we find names of places with the prefix *Don*, as *Dun*dalk, *Don*egal, and *Don*aghadee. This last place has a sound remarkably Hebrew, and transliterated becomes Danhaghedee, "Dan, my witness." From ancient Scotia we pass over to modern Scotia. Here we have *Dum*fries, *Dum*barton, (in these the letter n becomes m before the labial), *Dundee*, and Aberdeen (mouth of the *Don*), and the river *Don*."

Oxonian, in his invaluable book "*Israel's Wanderings*," states: "The immigration succeeding that of the Tuatha de Dannans (literally, Tribe of the Danites) is the Milesian colony of tradition generally known as Scuit, Scoti, or Scots. Prof. Sullivan says: "As to Milesians or Scots, the whole current of our legends and chronicles brings them from Spain;" and O'Curry, vol. I., "The Tuatha de Danaan and the Milesians both belonged to the same race" (chap. 72); and in Vol. II., pp. 3, 51, Prof. O'Curry says: "It is stated in a very old copy of the *Book of Invasions*, and other ancient documents, that *it was the Mosaic law that the Milesians brought into Erin at their coming*, and that it had been learned and received from Moses in Egypt by Cae Cain Breathach, *who was himself an Israelite*." Here then, may easily have been a second and larger immigration of Israelites into Ireland, who, during the period of the Assyrian invasion, came by degrees across the Mediterranean through Spain, and then across the intervening part of the Atlantic. This may have contained the remainder of Dan. The name Fenian may very possibly be derived from Phœnians—Phœnicians."

Benjamin.

This Tribe, for the reason previously stated, was detached from the Kingdom of Israel and remained with the House of Judah up to the time of the Roman siege, at the temporary raising of which they escaped.

"How did Benjamin join their brethren in the Isles of the West?

"There are grounds for believing that representatives of Benjamin spread all over Asia Minor, and it is more than probable that the early Apostolic Churches were mainly the fruit of the reception of the truth by Benjamin, and of the work of St. Paul, himself "an Israelite of the tribe of Benjamin."

Quoting again from *Israel's Wanderings*, by Oxonian: "In the year A.D. 267, we are told by Professor Max Muller (*Lectures on the Science of Language*, Series I., p. 188), "the Goths made a raid from Europe to Asia, Galacia, and Cappadocia, and the Christian captives whom they carried back to the Danube, were the first to spread the light of the Gospel among the Goths." *This short sentence carries Benjamin half way to Britain.*"

"As regards the possibility of their accomplishing the second half of the journey, it is of interest to note that according to Sharon Turner's "*History of the Anglo-Saxons*," Vol I., pp. 137—140, some adventurous "Franks and Saxons" were transplanted from their homes by the Emperor Probus in the year 270, and were located by him *in the very place where captive Benjamin and the other Christians had been carried only three years before*. When, ten years later, these transplanted Franco-Saxons made themselves "*masters of many vessels*," and left the shores of the Black Sea, may it not easily have happened that a portion at least of the Christian captives of A.D. 267 made their escape with them? *This one fact would carry Benjamin the rest of the way* to the country where the other tribes were already settled.

"Benjamin is further identified with those particular Normans who entered Britain in 1066. "*Northmen*" or "*Normans*" was simply a name given to successive bands of adventurers from Scandinavia as they reached the countries of the south. *It was not the name of a race.*

"It is also of interest to note that the founders of the Russian Empire were the Norman tribe of *Rus*, under Ruric, and that *Rosh* was, in the Scripture genealogies, one of the families of Benjamin.

"In Creasy's "*Fifteen Decisive Battles of the World*" the following dates are given:—

"911. The French King cedes Neustria to Hrolf the Norman. *He and his army* of Scandinavian warriors *become the* ruling *class* of the population of the province, *which is called after them Normandy.*

"*Benjamin shall raven as a wolf.*" Listen to the words of Lord Macaulay : "*The Normans were the foremost race of Christendom.* Their *valour* and *ferocity* had made them conspicuous among the rovers whom Scandinavia had sent forth to ravage Western Europe. Their sails were long the terror of both coasts of the Channel. . . . Their chief fame was derived from their military exploits. Every country, from the Atlantic Ocean to the Dead Sea, witnessed the prodigies of their discipline and valour. *One Norman knight, at the head of a handful of warriors, scattered the Celts of Connaught. Another* founded the monarchy of the Two Sicilies, and *saw the Emperors both of the East and the West fly before his arms.*"

"At length, in 1066, came the battle of Hastings, fitly described as *one of the decisive battles of the world*, for it was this which realised the union of Israel in the Isles of the West.

"The special characteristic of Benjamin to "*raven like a wolf*" is applicable in a marked degree to these Normans. The cognizance of the Dukes of Normandy was a *Wolf*, and the Standard under which these Normans fought at this memorable battle was emblazoned with a *Wolf*."

A noticeable feature in the historical career of Benjamin is, that they alone of all the tribes of Israel were never uncovenanted. They remained faithful to the Mosaic Covenant when their brethren of the House of Israel were "cut off," or "divorced" from it; moreover, they accepted the New or Christian Covenant, which the House of Judah with whom they were then in alliance, not only refused, but crucified the Messiah, whom "Caiaphas . . . being high priest . . . prophesied that Jesus should die . . . not for the nation only, but that he might also gather together *into one the children of God* (the Ten Tribes) *that are scattered abroad*." John 11. 52.

Having thus traced the Lost Tribes of the House of Israel to the British Isles, the next step is to give

The Different Names

(Condensed from "Our Scythian Ancestors," by the late Colonel Gawler; "Historical, Ethnic, etc., Arguments," by Philo-Israel; and "Israel's Wanderings," by Oxonian.)

under which they were successively known from the time of their deportation to the present day

Originally called the *House of Israel*, they were sometimes spoken of as the House of "*Jacob*,"

"*Joseph*," or "*Ephraim*," and also as "*All Israel*," in the prophetical Scriptures.

The Kingdom of Israel is also known as *Beth Khumri*—the House of Omri*—the name applied by the Assyrian inscriptions to the House of Israel, as the following taken from the Nimroud Obelisk, now in the British Museum will show:—"The tribute of Jehu, the son of Khumri (Omri), silver, gold, bowls, vessels, goblets, and pitchers of gold, with sceptres for the King's hand: all these have I received." The recipient was Shalmaneser II., and the people Jehu ruled were the Khumri, whose capital and country (Samaria) many other inscriptions term "Beth Khumri."

Sir Henry Rawlinson says the ethnic name of "Gimiri" occurs in the Cuneiform records as the Semetic equivalent of the Aryan name Saka. The *Gimiri* of the Assyrian inscriptions were known to the Greeks by the name of *Cimmerioi*; to the Romans as *Cimbri*; and may be traced (about the seventh century, B.C.), to the *Crim*-ea, then to *Cimbri*-c Chersonese or Jutland, about B.C. 200 to *Cumber*-land in Britain, and finally as *Cymry* to Wales, to which they gave their own name *Cambri*-a. Professor Rawlinson, with Sharon Turner, admits the identity of the **Cymry of Wales** with the Cimbri of the Romans.

---

* Omri founded the kingdom of *Samaria*. Tirzah and Shechem having been the capitals before his time. His name is, in Hebrew, עמרי, commencing with that curious half-vowel, half-guttural sound ע with which Gomorrah begins. So too we have Gaza and Azzah (two transliterations of the same Hebrew name), represented by the modern Guzzeh. Hence the founder of Samaria might just as well appear under the form Gimri, or as on the Assyrian Inscriptions, **Khumri.** That, in fact, was the sound of his name.

—*Oxonian.*

The Lost House of Israel in the course of their wanderings after their departure from Samaria to Assyria, have also been discovered under the prophetic name of "Beth Isaac," or "House of Isaac." "In Isaac shall thy seed be called." In Amos (chapter 7), Israel and the House of Isaac, are used synonymously and as distinct from Judah.

Sakai or Saccæ is really derived from Itsahhak ("laughter") the initial I being dropped: hence Isaacites.

Herodotus states (6, cap. 64): "The Persians called all the Scythians Sakai."

Pliny (6, cap. 2), says that the Sakai who settled in Armenia are named "Saccassani."

Dr. Moore, in his book "*The Lost Tribes and the Saxons of the East and West*, &c.," p. 89, states: "Saca-suni (the name of these Sakai) is equivalent in Hebrew to 'the changed Saks,' not sons of Sak, but Saks that have altered their abode or character. . . . The name was applied first as simply *The Tribes*, perhaps adopted from themselves, but ultimately it came to signify 'bowman,' because they, *like the Ephraimites and the English** were so famous for the use of the bow."

Ptolemy mentions a Scythian people sprung from the Sakai named Saxones.

Sharon Turner, Vol. 1, book 2, cap. 1, says: "The Scythian tribes have become better known to us in recent periods under the name of Getæ or Goths."

Under this term of Getæ as a portion of the Scythian nation, Herodotus describes them (4, cap. 93), as "the most valiant and most just of the Thracians."

* *Italics by Ozonian.*

Abraham Ortellius, in his *Theatrum Orbis Terrarum*, states: "The inhabitants of Dacia, the Greeks call Daci, the Latines Getæ. . . . Iornandes saith that the Romans indifferently called them Daci or Gothi."

Christianity early took root among these Goths or Scythians. A Gothic bishop was present at the Council of Nice, A.D. 325.

Herodotus (4, cap. 6) says they called themselves "Scoloti," which the Greeks pronounced "Scuthi." The name is not unreasonably traced to the Hebrew סכות (the *Succoth*, "booths," of the A.V.), variously pronounced S'cos, or S'coth by the Ashkenazim or German Jews, and S'cot by the Sephardim or Spanish Jews.

The Scoti, or Scots, actually came to Ireland (Scotia Major) from Spain.

An Irish legend states that the people were called Scoti, "from their leader, Ebur Scot, or Ebur Scythian," *i.e.*, the Wandering Hebrew.

In Hebrew, as we have seen, Scot or Scoth means "booths" (see Gen. 33. 17) or temporary dwellings, and the dwellers in them would be Scothi, *i.e.*, wanderers.

The Rev. M. Sailman, a Jew, writing in 1818, in a book entitled "*Researches in the East : an Important Account of the Ten Tribes*," quotes Ortellius thus : he " notes the kingdom of *Arsareth*, where the Ten Tribes, retiring, took the name of 'Gauthei,' because, says he, they were very jealous of the glory of God."

Gimiri of the Babylon transcripts, says Sir H. Rawlinson, is the Semitic equivalent of the Aryan name of Saka. " The Sacæ (Sakai), or Scythians, first appear in the cuneiform inscriptions about 684 B.C."

The connection of the Scythians, Scots and Goths with Dan is to be noted: we have Scyths, Goths, and Danai in the Black Sea, Gothland and Dannemerk in the Baltic, Scots and Dannans in the British Isles.

To sum up these different names, we find the Ten Tribes known;
Scripturally as the House of Israel, Isaac, Jacob, Joseph, or Ephraim; whilst,
Historically we find them successively described as Beth Khumri, the House of Omri; Gimiri, Cimmeroi, Cimbri, Beth Isaac (or House of Isaac), Sakai, Saccassani, Sacasuni, Saks, Saxones. Again, as Scythians, Scoloti, Scoti (or Scots), Skuthai; Getæ (or Goths), and Daci (Danes); finally passing into these Islands as the Welsh Cymry, Scots, Angles, Saxons, Frisians, Danes, and Normans, now collectively spoken of as the English or British people.

It does not follow that because our Ancestors arrived in the British Isles at various times and under different names, that therefore they were a mixed race, any more than that the Jews were a mingled people on the day of Pentecost; when it is recorded (The Acts. 2. 5—12):

"Now there were dwelling at Jerusalem Jews, devout men, from every nation under heaven. . . .

"And they were all amazed and marvelled, saying, Behold, are not all these (the Apostles) which speak Galilæans."

"And how hear we, every man in our own language, wherein we were born?

"Parthians and Medes and Elamites, and the dwellers in Mesopotamia;

"In Judæa and Cappadocia, in Pontus and Asia, in Phrygia and Pamphylia, in Egypt, and in parts of Libya about Cyrene, and sojourners from Rome, both Jews and proselytes.

"Cretans and Arabians, we do hear them speaking in our tongues the mighty works of God."

With reference to the origin or derivation of the term British, the following is put forward, *merely as a suggestion*. "*B'rith*" in Hebrew means *Covenant*, and "*Ish*"=*man*; together B'rith-ish, which is almost the phonetic equivalent of British: Covenant Man—Covenant People, *which we are if descended from* Abraham.

It must further be remembered that the House of Israel will not be known as such in the latter days, because it is declared in Isaiah 65. 15,

"He shall call his *servants* by another name."

That this term "servants" is applied to the Ten Tribes, and not to the Jews, is apparent on referring to the context; vide verses 13—17, wherein the temporal condition of the two people is thus contrasted :

"Behold my servants shall eat, but ye shall be hungry: behold, my servants shall drink, but ye shall be thirsty : behold, my servants shall rejoice, but ye shall be ashamed :

"Behold my servants shall sing for joy of heart, but ye shall cry for sorrow of heart, and shall howl for vexation of spirit."

Language.

Isaiah 28. 11, "For with stammering lips and with another tongue will he speak to this people:" (*i.e.*, Ephraim, *vide* verse 1). *Ergo*, it is some other language than that which was spoken by the children of Israel in Palestine in the days of old. Formerly of course it was Hebrew, but that is now a dead language quite as much as Latin, and is only made use of even by the Jews for religious purposes, as in the Service of the Synagogue, etc; and as Bishop Titcomb has shown, when they abandon their faith, they generally give up the Hebrew language.

The Bible, "the national heirloom of the British people," was written, in the original; the Old Testament in Hebrew, and the New Testament in Greek. The translation as we now have it, is in "another tongue" and that of course English; necessarily the rendering of the true sense of the original language is somewhat faulty or "stammering," as proved by the need in recent years of a new or "revised version" of the Holy Scriptures.

It is recorded that the Jews, in the seventy years of the Babylonian captivity, forgot their mother tongue and it is well known that their descendants of the present day adopt the language of whatever country they live in. Is it not therefore somewhat unreasonable to expect, that their Brethren of the House of Israel should be speaking the Hebrew tongue to day, some 2600 years after the date of their Assyrian captivity?

It is now universally admitted by leading philologists that language is not a test of Race, but only of social contact. **If it were not so**, the Jews who returned from Babylon ought, on the assumption that "language is the pedigree of race," to have been Chaldeans! The absurdity of such an assumption carries its own contradiction.

Seeing that the Jews forgot their own tongue during the seventy years' captivity, and adopted the Chaldean language instead; doubtless the Ten Tribes as rightly conjectured by the Rev. Robert Douglas, would all the more adopt the language of the Medes, or old Armenian, which as Max Müller, Klaproth, Neumann, Sir H. Rawlinson, and others have shown, was of the Aryan or Indo-European, and not of the Semitic type of language. Language, therefore, is *not* a pedigree of race.

It is sometimes asserted that our language is of Teutonic origin; but is it so? The idiom and grammar of both languages are entirely different. The complex genders and terminations as also the position of the verb at the close of the sentence, shows conclusively that there is a great difference between the German and our own tongue. But with Hebrew and English the case is exactly the opposite, for they both agree, as will readily be seen on translating a sentence from one language into the other.

Latham's *Germania of Tacitus*, p. 116, states that " the mother tongue of the present English—Anglo-Saxon—is extinct on the continent, wholly replaced by high German as the literary language, and by Platt-Deutsch as the speech of the country people."

Traces of the Hebrew language can still be found among us; notably in the Welsh dialect, which is full of Hebrew words and idioms. The British tongue is also idiomatically Hebrew. Tyndal, in prefacing his translation of the Bible, says, " The properties of the Hebrew tongue agree a thousand times more with the English than with the Latin."

Finally, it is patent to every one at the present time, that if there is a language that bids fair to become the international medium of communication between the peoples of the whole world, it is the English tongue. This is in accordance with the prediction of Zephaniah 3. 9.

Religion.

Up to the time of the disruption of the Israelitish nation under Rehoboam, all the people observed the Mosaic law. After the division, however, the Ten Tribes under the influence of Jeroboam and his successors, gradually forsook the religion of their forefathers and became idolators. This sin was the cause of their punishment, for we read in Hosea 13: 1, " When Ephraim . . . became guilty in Baal, he died," and according to the same prophet (chap. 1, 4), " I . . . will cause the *kingdom of the house of Israel*[*] to cease," and so they became (verse 9) " Lo-ammi (not my people) : for ye are not my people, and I will not be your God." In other words, they were to appear like the people among whom their lot was cast—*Gentiles* —a term which distinguishes between the Chosen

[*] It is singular that this is the only passage in the Bible where this expression occurs.

People, and the rest of the nations who were not in covenant with God under the law of Moses.

On the other hand of the Jews it is said, "But I will have mercy upon the house of Judah," (verse 7), a promise which was fulfilled by their restoration from the Babylonian captivity.

It is therefore necessary, for the sake of clearness and the proper understanding of this argument, to clearly distinguish between the two Covenants.

The Mosaic Covenant

was *conditional*, as stated in Exod. 19. 5—8, "Now therefore, if ye will obey my voice indeed, and keep my covenant, then ye shall be a peculiar treasure unto me from all peoples: for all the earth is mine: and ye shall be unto me a kingdom of priests, and an holy nation.

"And all the people answered together, and said, All that the Lord hath spoken we will do."

The observance or non-observance of this Covenant therefore entailed the consequent blessings or curses enumerated in Deuteronomy, on the people throughout their generations.

The House of Israel was ultimately "divorced" from this Mosaic Covenant, as stated in Hos. 2. and Isa. 50. 1, but on repentance was to be remarried and brought under the New Covenant, as declared in Hos. 2. 14, 23. Isa. 54, and Jer. 31.

The Abrahamic Covenant.

was *absolutely unconditional*, and wholly unconnected with the Mosaic Covenant.

"Now this I say: a covenant confirmed beforehand by God, the law, which came four hundred and thirty years after doth not disannul, so as to make the promise of none effect " (Gal. 3. 17).

St. Paul is at particular pains to explain and emphasise the difference between the two Covenants. He states that Christ is,

"The Mediator of a better covenant, which hath been enacted upon better promises." "Not according to the covenant that I made with their fathers . . . For they continued not in my covenant."

It was also of the nature of a testament or will of no effect until the death of the Testator (Heb. 9. 15, 16). It is mentioned in Gal. 3. 16—29: "Now to Abraham were the promises spoken, and to his seed. He said not, And to seeds, as of many: but as of one, And to thy seed, which is Christ."

So long, therefore, as Israel remained under the law, they were in the position of minors (Gal. 4. 1—7), but by the death of the Testator—Christ, the one seed—Israel the inheritor, comes of age and enters into possession of *the promises*, which were both of a *literal* and *spiritual* nature.

The whole argument of St. Paul, as set forth in the 4th, 8th, and 11th chapters of Romans being, that the Abrahamic blessings were made;

"Not in circumcision, but in uncircumcision : "

"For not through the law was the promise to Abraham or to his seed, that he should be heir of the world, but through the righteousness of faith."

"For this cause it is of faith, that it may be according to grace: to the end that the promise may be sure to all the seed; not to that only which is of the law (Judah), but to that also which is of the faith of Abraham, who is the father of us all."

"What shall we say then? That the Gentiles, (Lo-Ammi Israel) which followed not after righteousness, attained to righteousness, even the righteousness which is of faith, but (Judah) Israel, following after a law of righteousness, did not arrive at that law.

"Wherefore? Because they sought it not by faith, but as it were by works."

"For I bear them witness that they have a zeal for God, but not according to knowledge.

"For being ignorant of God's righteousness, and seeking to establish their own, they did not subject themselves to the righteousness of God.

"For Christ is the end of the law unto righteousness to every one that believeth."

"For I would not brethren, have you ignorant of this *mystery*, lest ye be wise in your own conceits, *that a hardening in part hath befallen Israel* (the Jews), *until the fulness of the Gentiles* ("Lo-Ammi" Ten Tribed Israel *) be come in;' and so *all* (the Twelve Tribes of) Israel shall be saved."

Whilst this New Covenant was to be made with "the House of Israel and the House of Judah;' it is noteworthy that in recapitulating this promise (Heb. 8. 10), the House of Israel only is mentioned and Judah omitted, inferentially proving that the former was to come under it first. †

* See note on this passage on page 41 under the heading of "The Birthright Blessings.")

† It is obvious that if the *Old* Covenant was not made with Gentiles of Japhetic or Hamitic origin, neither could the *New* Covenant be made with them.

As *a matter of fact*, the Jews remain under the Mosaic Covenant unto this day, and according to Zechariah will continue to do so until the Second Advent, when "they shall look unto him whom they (the Jews) have pierced and they shall mourn for him, as one mourneth for his only son" (Chap. 12. 10, also John 19. 37).

The House of Israel therefore, is to be found in the latter days under the Christian covenant.

It may also be as well perhaps to refer here to the statement of St. Paul in Gal. 3. 28—

"There can be neither Jew nor Greek, there can be neither bond nor free, there can no male and female: for ye are all one man in Christ Jesus.

"And if ye are Christ's, then are ye Abraham's seed, heirs according to promise."

The plain meaning of this passage is, that whilst Christianity puts all who accept its precepts on a basis of "*spiritual*" or individual equality, it does not abolish *racial*, any more than it does *sexual* distinction.

A Frenchman, Hindoo, or Hottentot may accept Christianity, and thus become "the seed of Abraham by faith;" but that does not confer *racial* descent from Abraham, which we Englishmen claim.

The material blessings which we enjoy are due to the faithfulness of God to "His promises, made to our forefathers Abraham, Isaac, and Jacob," as we are so beautifully reminded in our Church Service every Sunday. Would that the Clergy and Congregation of our National Church realised the *literal* meaning of the words put into their mouths by the Book of Common Prayer surely they would join in the service with a heartfelt devotion and pleasure unknown to all, except those who realise their literal Israelitish descent.

This Abrahamic covenant was divided, so that the,

" Birthright was given unto the sons of Joseph the son of Israel. . . .

" For Judah prevailed above his brethren, and of him came the prince, but the birthright was Joseph's." 1 Chron. 5. 1-2.

Therefore to Judah was given the Sceptre and from him was to come the Messiah, the promised "Seed "—Christ; whilst to Joseph and his descendants was bequeathed the temporal blessings.

The Birthright Blessings

we claim as our national heritage, but permit other nations to share with us by virtue of our Free Trade: "Made in Germany" is a familiar commercial illustration of this fact, as some of our Manufacturers find to their cost.

"And Jacob called unto his sons, and said: Gather yourselves together, that I may tell you that which shall befall you in the "*latter days.*" (Gen. 48. 1).

It will be remembered that Joseph had previously brought his two sons that they might receive his father's blessing, as recorded in the preceding chapter of Genesis.

" And Israel strengthened himself, and sat upon the bed.

"And Jacob said unto Joseph, . . .

"And now thy two sons, which were born unto thee in the land of Egypt before I came unto thee into Egypt, are mine; Ephraim and Manasseh even as Reuben and Simeon, shall be mine. . .

"The angel which hath redeemed me from all evil, bless the lads; and let my name (*Israel*) be named on them, and the name of my fathers Abraham and Isaac; and let them grow into a multitude in the midst of the earth."

The aged Patriarch then proceeds to cross his hands, so that the greater blessing falls on the younger son Ephraim; predicting that his seed shall become

A Mighty Empire, and a Company of Nations.

"And his seed shall become a multitude of nations." *

"A nation and a company of nations shall be of thee" (Gen. 35. 11).

"Sing with gladness for Jacob and shout for the chief of the nations" (Jer. 31. 7).

The context shows that this refers to the House of Israel—"Ephraim—my firstborn" (verse 9).

* Or as it is stated in the margin, a "*fulness of the nations.*—Hebrew " Goyim."

"The word here translated 'nations' is in Hebrew *goyim*, and is thus explained in the Preface to the Revised Version of the Bible. "The Hebrew word *goyim* (nations), which is applied to the nations of Canaan dispossessed by the Hebrews, and then also to the surrounding nations among whom the people of Israel were afterwards dispersed, acquired in later times a moral significance, which is represented in the Authorised Version by the rendering 'heathen or Gentiles.' In other words, the House of Israel, when 'divorced from the law,' became like the 'heathen' or 'Gentiles' in the eyes of their brethren of the house of Judah."

"The children of thy bereavement shall say in thine ears, the place is too strait for me : give place to me that I may dwell" (Isaiah 49. 20).

The seed of Ephraim, or the House of Joseph, was therefore to become a "a company of *goyim*," or Gentile nations, not under the Mosaic law. †

The British Isles are the only ones that will meet the requirements of prophecy, and being too small to hold the continually increasing population, the people emigrate to the Colonies, founding "daughter nations of the Old Mother in the West." Thus fulfilling the prediction of our forefather Israel, that "Joseph is a fruitful bough by a fountain, his branches (*margin*—daughters) run over the wall." In other words, the British people of the House of Joseph, encircled by the walls of the sea, have spread all over the world.

Great Britain, with her Colonies and Dependencies, form the greatest Empire the world has ever seen, and when Colonial Federation with the Mother country becomes an accomplished fact, they will literally form "a nation and a company of nations."

Manasseh on the other hand was to become

A Great People.

"He also shall become a people, and he also shall be great."

America, (Brother Jonathan) can be easily recognised as fulfilling the destiny of Manasseh, being admittedly as they themselves claim to be, a "great people." They further fulfil the words

† This argument is very ably worked out by Dr. Aldersmith in his valuable book, "*The Fulness of the Nations.*"

of Isaiah by being the only Colony lost to the Mother Country. This is predicted by Isaiah.

"The children which thou shalt have, after thou hast lost the other, shall say again in thy ears, The place is too strait for me: give place to me that I may dwell." (Chap. 49. 20, A.V.)

It is obvious that the blessings to the sons of Joseph were not fulfilled in the first settlement of the children of Israel in Palestine, neither can they be realised after the final restoration of all the Tribes to the Holy Land; because when that takes place, God declares, according to the Prophet Ezekiel (37. 22), that not only the House of Israel —or Joseph—but also the House of Judah shall then be "one nation in the land upon the mountains of Israel; and one king shall be king to them all and they shall be no more two nations, neither shall they be divided into two kingdoms any more at all," therefore these blessings must have their accomplishment in this the Christian dispensation.

A Multitudinous Race.

"I will make thy (Abraham's) seed as the dust of the earth" (Gen. 13. 16).

"I will multiply thy seed as the stars of the heaven and as the sand which is upon the sea shore" (Gen. 22, 17).

This promise to Abraham, was confirmed to Ephraim and Manasseh, the heads of the subdivided House of Joseph: and of them it was predicted that they should "increase as fishes do increase." A further reference to Hosea 1. 9—11, will show that this promise was to take effect *after* the children of Israel were "outcast" from the Mosaic covenant and their land, but *previous* to their joint return with Judah to Palestine.

It is a fact that our population increases at a faster rate than that of any other nation on the face of the earth, as a reference to any modern statistics will readily prove.

Possessing the Gates of their Enemies.

"And thy seed shall possess the gate of his enemies" (Gen. 22. 17).

This is notably fulfilled by England, in possession of Gibraltar, Malta, Aden, Galle, Singapore, Hong-Kong, etc., thereby dominating by holding these and other strategic positions all over the world, the enemies' lands in which they are placed.

The late Bishop Patrick, commenting on this passage, observes : "These gates are Cities, consequently the country ; for the gates being taken, the cities are entered, and the cities surrendered ; the country is conquered."

Dwelling in the Appointed Place.
In Safety—Alone.

"And I will appoint a place for my people Israel,* and will plant them, that they may dwell in thine own place, and be moved no more ; neither

---

* Canon Farrar says in his comment on 2 Kings 9. 6, in the Expositor's Bible Series—"The expression is remarkable as showing how completely the prerogative of the Chosen People was supposed to rest with the Ten Tribes, as the most important representatives of the seed of Abraham."

shall the children of wickedness afflict them any more, as at the first" (2 Sam. 7. 10).

This obviously could not refer to Samaria as they were carried into captivity from thence, becoming "*wanderers among the nations*" (Hos. 9. 17), yet not lost because Amos says:

"I will sift the house of Israel among all the nations, like as corn is sifted in a sieve, yet shall not the least grain fall upon the earth."

"All the sinners of my people shall die by the sword, which say, The evil shall not overtake or prevent us" (Chap. 9. 10).

A renewal of our forefathers' experience when they "tempted him in the wilderness," after the Exodus, with the result that the sinners were destroyed, but the faithful *remnant* saved.

Ultimately the House of Israel as predicted by Hosea (2. 14), was to be allured "into the wilderness." Isaiah too declares:

"Keep silence before me, O Islands and let the peoples renew their strength" (41. 1).

"Listen, O Isles, unto me: and hearken, ye peoples, from far" (49. 1).

From these passages, and for reasons previously given, it is obvious that only the British Isles can be therein indicated.

"Lo it is a people that dwell alone" (Num. 23. 9), at the time of their "last end" (verse 10). Geographically we "dwell alone" in these Islands in a way that Israel of old certainly never did in Palestine: a further light is thrown on the meaning in which perhaps this passage can be bettter understood, in

1 Kings 8. 53, "For thou didst separate them from among all the peoples of the earth, to be *thine inheritance.*"

Witness the blind testimony of our National Church Service, wherein the Congregation in reply to the words of the Minister—"O Lord save thy people," respond: "And bless *thine inheritance.*" Truly God has done so, in every sense of the word.

That the appointed place was promised to Israel and not Judah, is self-evident in the light of its fulfilment. Moreover, this is confirmed by a reference to the prophecy of Balaam, which applies to the people in a state of blessedness and prosperity—*not adversity*—in the latter days.

"Who can count the dust of Jacob,
  Or number the fourth part of Israel.
  Let me die the death of the righteous.
  And let my last end be like his."

Is obviously as inapplicable to the Jews, as it is applicable to the vast British population.

The comforting assurance too of freedom from foreign invasion; a promise confirmed by actual experience, must naturally be a source of great comfort and peace of mind in times of political anxiety, and makes it the more imperative to all who realise the literal application of this blessing to our nation, to spread the knowledge of our identity with Israel throughout the length and breadth of the Empire.

A Free Country.

"And if a stranger sojourn with thee in your land, ye shall not do him wrong."

"The stranger that sojourneth with you shall be unto you as the home-born among you, and thou shalt love him as thyself; *for ye were strangers in the land of Egypt*" (Lev. 19. 33—34).

It is open to Foreigners the wide world over to take up their abode with us; enjoying the same privileges and blessings, and on becoming naturalised, of attaining to the highest Offices of State, etc. Isaiah 56. 3—8 contains special references on this subject.

Anglo-Israelites.

"Who is blind, but my servant, or deaf, as my messenger that I send?" (Isaiah 42. 19.)

"One shall say, I am the Lord's; and another shall call himself by the name of Jacob; and another shall . . . surname himself by the name of Israel" (Isa. 44. 5).

"And it shall come to pass that, in the place where it was said unto them, Ye are not my people, it shall be said unto them, Ye are the sons of the living God" (Hos. 1. 10).*

In spite of explicit statements in the Bible, there are millions of British people who are blind to their Israelitish origin, and apparently deaf to all explanation on the subject. On the other hand, it is gratifying to know that there is a large and constantly increasing body of Her Majesty's subjects who are proud to call themselves Israelites, and as such will be ultimately recognised by the whole world.

* It is noteworthy that this prediction is to be fulfilled to the House of Israel, *after* they had been outcast from their land, and from the Mosaic Covenant, vide, verses 4—9, but *before* the final return *accompanied by* their brethren of Judah, to Palestine, verse 11.

The Dominion of the Sea.

"His seed shall be in many waters" (Numbers 24. 7).

This prophecy of Balaam was to be fulfilled in the "latter days" (verse 15). If there is a people to whom this passage pre-eminently applies, it is the British Nation, the greatest naval and commercial power in the world's history. Truly it may be said that we enjoy "the blessings of the deep that coucheth beneath" (Gen. 49. 25), as in addition to the "harvest of the sea,"—two-thirds of the shipping trade is in our hands—the water serves as a natural defence for our island home.

Under Divine Protection.

"No weapon formed against thee shall prosper" (Isaiah 54. 17).

In times of great political anxiety, when possibly the best interests of the country may be jeopardised by any false political movement on the part of our Government; the above words are most comforting, and enable one to realise in a practical manner the prophetical injunction, "Thou wilt keep him in perfect peace, whose mind is stayed on thee" (Isa. 26. 3). This does not mean of course that we are to sit still and do nothing in times of national emergency, but, having done all in our power to strengthen our position, we must trust to Providence to pull us through our difficulties and troubles.

The Missionary People.

"Ye are my witnesses, saith the Lord; and my servant, whom I have chosen"

"The people which I formed for myself, that they might set forth my praise" (Isaiah 43. 10, 21.)

"In days to come shall Jacob take root; Israel shall blossom and bud: and they shall fill the face of the world with fruit* (Isaiah 27. 6).

"Therefore I say unto you (Jews), The kingdom of God shall be taken away from you, and shall be given to a nation bringing forth the fruits thereof." (Matthew 21. 43).

The English as the Missionary people of the world, are performing the duty of Israel. If this fact was realised, what a powerful argument the Pulpit would have when appealing for funds to support the various Missionary Societies maintained by the inhabitants of these Islands.

Collection boxes may owe their origin to the suggestion contained in 2 Kings. 12. 9?

"The priest took a chest, and bored a hole in the lid of it, and set it beside the altar, on the right side as one cometh into the house of the Lord: and the priests that kept the door put therein all the money that was brought into the house of the Lord."

India.

"He hath shewed his people the power of His works, in giving them the heritage of the heathen" (Psalm 111. 6, A.V.)

Our magnificent Heathen Empire is given us in a very literal manner, for the people of India maintain at their own cost, the army with which we keep their country in subjection.

* Ephraim, means fruitful.

The conquest of India is predicted in Isaiah 41. 2—7: it is noticeable that whilst other invaders of India passed through Afghanistan, we, the seed of Abraham, went "even by a way which he had not gone by his feet" (ver. 3) *i.e.*, by the sea which carried us there.

Africa

too, bids fair to be another illustration of this prophecy.

An Invincible Army and Navy.

" The shield of his mighty men is made red; the valiant men are in scarlet." Nahum 2. 3.

The colour of our national uniform.

" Five of you shall chase an hundred, and an hundred of you shall chase ten thousand; and your enemies shall fall before you by the sword." Lev. 26. 8.

This is a conditional promise made, and to be always fulfilled to, Israel, " If ye walk in my statutes, and keep my commandments, and do them " (Lev. 26. 3). Christ having fulfilled the law for us, and we as a nation having been brought under the New Covenant which was to be made with the House of Israel, are now "obedient," and have for centuries past enjoyed the benefits of this great blessing.

British pluck is proverbial, and the conquest of India is an instance of victory obtained against tremendous odds; but how few realise the true source of our naval and military successes.

What might not be the effect upon our Soldiers and Sailors, if, realising their Israelitish origin, the

Chaplains to the Forces, like their Hebrew predecessors, the Priests of old, were to exhort the men before going into action, in accordance with the message contained in Deuteronomy 20. 1—4?

"When thou goest forth to a battle against thine enemies, and seest horses, and chariots, and a people more than thou, thou shalt not be afraid of them: for the Lord thy God is with thee, which brought thee up out of the land of Egypt.

"And it shall be, when ye draw nigh unto the battle, that the priest shall approach and speak unto the people,

"And shall say unto them, Hear, O Israel, ye draw nigh this day unto battle against your enemies: let not your heart be faint; fear not, nor tremble, neither be ye affrighted at them; for the Lord your God is he that goeth with you, to fight for you against your enemies, to save you."

Who could stand against a Force animated with courage inspired from such a source?

The "British square"; the favorite formation of our Troops, is but a continuation of the marching order of our Hebrew Forefathers as detailed in the second chapter of Numbers.

Foreign Loans.

"Thou shalt lend unto many nations, but thou shalt not borrow; and thou shalt rule over many nations, but they shall not rule over thee" (Deut. 15. 6).

A glance at the Money Market columns of the Daily Papers will show that we have lent money to nearly every nation in the world, whilst we ourselves have borrowed of none.

It is a mistake to suppose as so many do, that the Jews are the money lending people of the world. It is true that great Jewish firms like the Rothschilds for instance, act as Agents in raising Foreign Loans in this country, but it is the British Public who find the money by subscribing for them, and not the Jews.

We also rule over Frenchmen in Canada, Spaniards in Gibraltar, Italians in Malta, Dutchmen in South Africa,* Chinese in Hong Kong, etc. but we ourselves on the other hand are not ruled over by anyone.

Putting Down Slavery and Oppression.

"Thou shalt not deliver unto his master a servant which is escaped from his master unto thee: he shall dwell with thee, in the midst of thee, in the place which he shall choose within one of thy gates, where it liketh him best: thou shalt not oppress him." (Deut. 23. 15).

"Is not this the fast that I have chosen? to loose the bonds of wickedness, to undo the bands of the yoke, and to let the oppressed go free, and that ye break every yoke?

"Is it not to deal thy bread to the hungry, and that thou bring the poor that are cast out to thy house? when thou seest the naked, that thou cover him; and that thou hide not thyself from thine own flesh?" (Isaiah 58. 6—7).

* The rule of President Kruger at Pretoria, over the South African Republic, is but a permissive form of Government: practically existing during the pleasure of the Colonial Office.

For years this country has kept a portion of its Navy engaged in suppresing the Slave trade in all parts of the world. Directly a poor runaway slave steps on board a British Man of War, he is a free man. May not our valuable possessions in Africa, the home of the Slave, be God's gift to us for thus obeying His commands?

Downtrodden and oppressed races all over the world constantly appeal to this country for sympathy and help: the Expedition to Ashanti on the Gold Coast is a recent example of our beneficent interference in the cause of humanity.

A Blessing to other Nations.

" In thy seed shall all the nations of the earth be blessed" (Gen. 22: 18).

Whether regarded from a religious point of view, as evidenced by our missionary efforts, or from a political standpoint as demonstrated by our commercial enterprise and free trade; wherever our people go, there they carry prosperity with them, to the mutual advantage of everyone with whom they come in contact.

A Sabbath Keeping People.

" The children of Israel shall keep my Sabbaths throughout their generations, for a perpetual covenant. It is a sign between me and the children of Israel for ever" (Exod. 31. 16—17).

Also Exod. 20. 2—17, containing the Ten Commandments.

" For this is your wisdom and your understanding in the sight of the peoples, which shall hear all these statutes, and say, Surely this great nation is a wise and understanding people.

"For what great nation is there, that hath God so nigh unto them, as the Lord our God is whensoever we call upon Him?

"And what great nation is there, that hath statutes and judgments so righteous as all this law, which I set before you this day?" (Deut. 4. 6—8).

There are only three people who strictly keep the Sabbath, nationally and by law—the Jews, the English, and the Americans. No other nation, not even the Germans, keep the Sabbath entirely sacred.

Our National Church too, is the only Church in the world, which has the Ten Commandments set up in the Chancel, in accordance with the directions contained in the Rubric, "where they can be best seen and read of the people." It is a matter for sincere regret, that owing to architectural or ritualistic notions, the Two Tables are now too often superseded by the Reredos, which no matter how costly or beautiful as a work of art, is mere dross compared to the Ten Commandments, specially given as they were to us, the Chosen People.

The Union of Church and State.

"And Moses chose able men out of all Israel, and made them heads over the people, rulers of thousands, rulers of hundreds, rulers of fifties, and rulers of tens." (Exodus 18. 25).

See also chap. 24. 1, 11; where the elders of the people are called "nobles."

The Priests were likewise associated with Moses in the exercise of administrative and judicial functions. (2 Chron. 19.) This form of administration is now continued amongst us, by the existence of the House of Lords, * in which the Archbishops and Bishops sit as Spiritual Peers—and the House of Commons, which includes the representatives of the people. All laws made by them are promulgated in the name of the Queen, who is the Head of the Church and the State.

Until quite recently it was the custom to appoint Clergymen as Justices of the Peace.

It is also interesting to note that the reigning Monarch of Britain is by inheritance a Canon of St. David's Cathedral. Her Majesty's Stall there is always kept ready for her use.

* Would the present outcry for the abolition of the House of Lords have arisen, if we had adhered to Life, instead of Hereditary Peerages? "Originally the dignity of "'Earl,' or erl (Saxon, eorl), was an honorary title of distinction given to noblemen. The term originated with the nations of the North of Europe, who applied the title of jarl (pronounced yarl) to chieftains of the highest rank, having powers of a viceroy in the administration of justice . . . . It was introduced into England by the founders of the Saxon Heptarchy, and then applied to the nobles generally. . . The earls who presided over the courts of justice and public meetings of the district or shire entrusted to their management, were further distinguished by the title of 'ealdormen.' . . . . This title, at the time of the conquest, fell into disuse, and these Saxon governors of shires were all called 'earls.' This title remained the highest of rank in England till the latter part of the fourteenth century, when the dignities of duke and marquis were introduced, the holders of which took precedence over earls." ("Beeton's Dictionary of Universal Information," article: Earl, page 673).

The derivation of the word "elder," as given in "Chambers' Etymological English Dictionary," is as follows:—"Elder, adj. older; Anglo-Saxon, ealdor, comp. of eald, old. Of the word 'old,' Anglo-Saxon, eald." The elders, ealdormen, or earls, were, therefore, the seniors or chief men of the Saxon Heptarchy, the hereditary nobility of the Tribes, and Moses was particularly directed in Numbers 11. 16, to choose only those who were "elders of Israel," whom "he knew to be the elders of the people," and "officers over them," "to stand in the tabernacle of the congregation with Moses."—Quoted in "*The Banner of Israel*"

Formerly many Cathedrals and Churches in these Islands possessed a "Right of Sanctuary" (Exodus 21. 13), but with the altered condition of the times this old privilege has fallen into disuse.

The creation of County, and District Councils, is also a return to the simple and more common sense Levitical custom of administering provincial and rural affairs by local Authorities: this is what we are led to expect by the Prophet Isaiah. (Chap. 1. 26) "I will restore thy judges as at the first, and thy counsellors as at the beginning."

Various Other Hebrew Customs.

are extant among us, such as the Law of Primogeniture, (Deut. 21. 17). Tithes, (Leviticus 27.30). Seven years statute of limitation, (Exodus 21). Division of the land into Hundreds and Tithings (Exodus 18. 21). The Judges going on Circuit (1 Samuel 7. 16). Putting the Stone. * (Zech. 12. 3), etc. How are these facts to be accounted for except on the supposition of our Hebrew origin?

Our Royal Family Descended from David.

" The sceptre shall not depart from Judah,
  Nor the ruler's staff from between his feet,
  Until Shiloh come" (Gen. 49. 8—10).

This promise was to have its fulfilment in the "*latter days*" (Gen. 49. 1).

In these days when the Democracy reigns supreme, it is sometimes remarked that the next century will see every Throne in Europe totter to

---

* "*The stone of burden* alludes to a practice, which Jerome reports to have prevailed in Judea, of lifting heavy stones, as a trial of strength; something akin to our 'putting the stone." Extract from The Holy Bible with Commentary: Edited by F. C. Cook, M.A., Canon of Exeter.

its fall. Whatever the future may have in store for other Royal Families, this certainly will not be the case with our own; for the simple reason that it is contrary to the plain and repeated declarations of Scripture.

At first David reigned only over Judah, but ultimately "*the kingdom*," which, according to 2 Sam. 2. 9, consisted of Ephraim, Benjamin, and *all* Israel,* was (*vide* next chapter) translated from the house of Saul to the house of David, who then reigned over both Israel and Judah.

This rule over the twelve-tribed nation continued until the division under Rehoboam, when "*the kingdom, . . . even ten tribes*," was taken from him and handed over to Jeroboam instead (1 Kings 11.35—36). One tribe of the kingdom, however—Benjamin, as the historical records of Ezra and Nehemiah prove—was lent to Judah "that David my servant may have a lamp alway before me in Jerusalem." David's descendants continued to rule over Judah and Israel—the latter as represented by Benjamin —up to the time of the Babylonish captivity, when the last king of Judah, in the person of Zedekiah, died in that city. *From that time to the present day the Jewish people have never had a king reigning over them.*

To all outward appearances, therefore, the Throne of David had ceased to exist 588 years before Christ: but had it?—Most certainly not.

It is remarkable that at the very time of the apparent extinction of the Royal Family, Jeremiah emphasized the prophetic promise to

* "*All Israel*" here, be it noted, did not include Judah.

David by repeating the same, as recorded in chapter 33. 25—26.

"Thus saith the Lord: If my covenant of day and night stand not, if I have not appointed the ordinances of heaven and earth; then will I cast away the seed of Jacob, and of David my servant, so that I will not take of his seed to be rulers over the seed of Abraham, Isaac and Jacob: for I will cause their captivity to return and will have mercy on them."

These prophecies cannot be applied to the House of Judah or the Jews; therefore that the Scriptures may be fulfilled, they must be realised in the House of Israel.

It is as certain as the Bible is true, that wherever Israel exists as a Nation, there the Royal Family reigning over it *must* be of Davidic descent, *by virtue of their position*, in accordance with the promises to David. This statement can be proved on prophetical, traditional, and historical grounds.

In Ezekiel 17. 22—24, it is stated:

"I will also take of the lofty top of the cedar, and will set it; I will crop off from the topmost of his young twigs *a tender one*, * and I will plant it upon an high mountain and eminent:

"In the mountain of the height of Israel will I plant it: and it shall bring forth boughs, and bear fruit, and be a goodly cedar; and under it shall dwell all fowl of every wing: in the shadow of the branches thereof shall they dwell.

"And all the trees of the field shall know that I the Lord have brought down the high tree, have

---

* Bishop Horsley says this implies feminine gender.

exalted the low tree, have dried up the green tree, and have made the dry tree to flourish: I the Lord have spoken and have done it."

Also in chap. 21. 25—27, it is declared:

" And thou, O deadly wounded wicked one, this prince of Israel.

" Remove the mitre, and take off the crown: the shall be no more the same: exalt that which is low, and abase that which is high.

"I will overturn, overturn, overturn it: this also shall be no more, until he comes whose right it is; and I will give it to him."

The interpretation of these passages is as follows:—"The cedar tree," is the Royal House of David; "the lofty top," is the reigning member of it; "the tender one," or "twig," is the daughter of Zedekiah; which was planted "in the mountain of Israel." This mountain or nation could not refer to Judah, as they have never had a king of their own reigning over them since Zedekiah: it must therefore refer to the other House of Israel—the Ten Tribes. Judah who was at that time flourishing as a "green tree," has since "dried up" as a nation; whilst Israel, the then "dry tree," is now "flourishing" as the British nation. The Throne of Jehoiakim, Jehoiakin, and Zedekiah was "overturned" from the Jewish to the Israelitish nation, being no more in the "same" male line but the dynasty was to be continued in the female branch: the House of Israel, then "low," is now "exalted," whilst the House of Judah is "abased" from its high position and will remain so "until He (Christ) comes, whose right it is."

How can the footsteps of "the tender one," Zedekiah's daughter be traced?

It is recorded of Jeremiah that his mission was (chap. 1. 10), "to pluck up and to break down" and also "to build and to plant," "the nations." Special protection was vouchsafed him until he had accomplished his mission (chap. 1. 17—19). Jeremiah saw the overthrow of Judah; it therefore remained for him (chap. 3. 11—12) to "Go, and proclaim these words towards the *north* and say, return thou *backsliding* Israel . . . for I am merciful, saith the Lord."

The last account that we have of Jeremiah is, that in company with Zedekiah's daughters, he was taken against his will, down to Tahpanhes * in Egypt (chap. 43. 5—7), about B.C. 583. The Jews who accompanied him were warned that none should return "save such as shall escape" (chap. 44. 14). There are strong grounds for believing that Jeremiah took advantage of the Danites trading in company with the Phœnicians in the ports of Tyre, Egypt, Greece and the Isles of the Sea to escape to Ireland, as will be shown by the following statements:

One of the most prominent characters in Ancient Irish history is one Ollam Fodhla, † pronounced

---

* The Ruins of the Palace at Tahpanhes, have been found by the noted Mr. Flinders Petrie, and the site is known as "the Castle of the Jew's Daughter."

† The historic fame of Ollam Fola has been recognised by placing his medallion in basso-relievo with those of Moses and other great legislators on the interior of the Dome of the Four Courts in Dublin. Jeremiah or Jerry is, as is well

Ollav Fola. It has fallen to the lot of the late Rev. F. R. A. Glover, M.A., formerly chaplain to the Consul at Cologne, in his valuable work, entitled *"England, the Remnant of Judah, and the Israel of Ephraim, &c.,"* to identify Ollam Fodhla with Jeremiah. The Rev. Mr. Glover states, on p. 19 (quoting from the *"Annals of the Four Masters,"* p. 412): "Amongst the most celebrated kings of Ulster, who also reigned as monarchs of Ireland, was Ollam Fodhla, or Ollav Fola, the famous Legislator, whose reign is placed by Tigernach, O'Flaherty, and others about seven centuries before the Christian era. He founded the Conventions of Tara." "This," continues Mr. Glover, "is that Eocaid - Ollambh - Fodhla - Heremon - Ardrigh of Tara,* of whom the *"Chronicles of Eri"* (vol. 2, pp. 70, 85, 91, 116), make such ample and honourable mention."

Dr. Kelly, Professor of History at Maynooth, in his *Cambrensis Eversus* (vol. 1, p. 431), is quoted by Mr. Glover to the effect that Eochaid Heremon "gave Ulster to Ollam Fola." This name, therefore, given in the *Chronicles of Eri*, shows that two titles have been rolled into one, and includes in fact a King and his Minister.

This deduction is confirmed by the derivation of the names, which are of Hebrew origin. A Hebrew friend wrote to Mr. Glover thus: "If known, a common name in Ireland. It was Ollam Fola also that appointed a chieftain over every cantred, i.e., hundred; and a Brughaidh, i.e., a farmer, over every townland, who were all to serve the King of Ireland."—Quoted by E. A. Cornwall in his book, "The tomb of Ollamh Fodhla," p. 24.

* Eochaid means Historian; Ollam, Learned man; Fola, either Destiny or Learned: Heremon, King; Ardrigh, Head King or Pentarch. So Heremon was the King and Ollam Fola the Wise Man and Legislator, i.e., Prime Minister.

the word 'Ollam' was spoken as relating to a man, it would simply imply that he was a possessor of hidden secrets or knowledge which was not common to man generally," *i.e.*, a Prophet. Fola, according to a Celtic Dictionary, means "revealing," *i.e.*, a "revealer," or the equivalent of the Hebrew *fla*, which is used of all that is "wonderful." Ollam Fola was therefore known to the Ancient Irish, as the learned Hebrew Revealer or Hebrew Prophet. Eochaid-Heremon-Ardri, on the otherhand, was the name of the King. This Ollam Fola established at Tara a Mur-Ollamin, which is correctly "The Precinct of the Ollams," and known as Meralmin, being a perversion of Mur-Ollamin, *i.e.*, the School of the Prophets. According to the *Annals of the Four Masters*, p. 293, "Tara was also the building called Mur-Ollam-ham, or House of the Learned, in which resided the bards, brehons, and other learned men."

Tara, so long identified with the ancient annals of Ireland, is practically identical with the Hebrew title Torah, the Law. Mr. Glover states that "King Cimboath of Ulster—the certainty of whose epoch all seem to accept—died B.C. 353. Ollam Fola is stated to have preceded him by 230 years. Thus 353 + 230 = 583 B.C., the certainly known date of the Prophet Jeremiah subsequent to his departure from Judea."

In chap. x. of his most interesting book, Mr. Glover, through information gleaned from a poem composed by one Amergin, Chief Bard to King Dermod, Monarch of Ireland in the Sixth Century, as recounted in the "*Annals of the Four Masters*" (p. 294), relates how an Eastern Princess, "the daughter of Pharaoh," "Tephi" (in Hebrew a pet name, like Violet), the most beautiful, was married to "the gentle Heremon," who "all his promises to her he fulfilled," and who was eventually buried in a Tomb, of which it is stated "the length and breadth was *sixty* feet of exact measure," "and from her it was named Tea-mur." This is the "Great Mergech" * at Tara Hill, a term which in Hebrew means "a resting-place, or repository." †

This Eochaid Heremon was a Prince of the Tuatha de Danaan, or Tribe of Danites, and by his union with this Princess—whom by reason of her history, name, and the Hebrew origin of the terms applied to her residence, tomb, and last but not least her guardian, we reasonably identify as Zedekiah's daughter—the sovereignty was transferred from the House of Judah to the House of Israel as represented by the Tribe of Dan. Thus the continuity of the Throne and Seed of David, as also the Sceptre of Judah is maintained; because Her Most Gracious Majesty the Queen traces her pedigree back through the Scotch and Irish kings.

The current theological explanation that the 'Sceptre departed from Judah when Christ came,' will not meet the requirements of prophecy; which in unmistakable terms states that David should never want an heir to sit on his throne, whereas, as a matter of fact, Zedekiah the last king over the House of Judah, died in Babylon nearly 600 years

* Pronounced Merragh.

† There is a well known tradition in Ireland that "the Jews' Ark" is hidden in the Hill of Tara, County Meath, if this is so, it is probable that the Tables of the Law, are likewise therein.

before the advent of Christ, since which time there has been no descendant of David reigning as King over the House of Judah. Herod was an Idumæan and the Jews themselves said, in the time of our Lord 'We have no king but Cæsar.' "

If on the other hand the Anglo-Israelite theory is correct, then the promise has been fulfilled by the transference of the Sceptre to the House of Israel; and a text, the fulfilment of which has raised so much difficulty and controversy, is easily and readily explained.

Accepting the above explanation, how impressive and full of meaning is the Prayer of our National Church, taken from the Collect in the " Service for the Twentieth day of June," "let there never be one wanting in her house to succeed her in the government of this United Kingdom., that our posterity may see her children's children, and *peace upon Israel. So we that are thy people, and sheep of thy pasture*, shall give thee thanks *for ever*." If we are not the *literal* people of Israel, what in the name of common sense is the meaning of such a petition?

" Thy father's sons shall bow down before thee." Whenever loyal subjects meet members of the Royal Family, they make obeisance to them.

Finally, the Royal Arms, which consist of the crowned Lion of Judah, represent the Royal Family by virtue of their Davidic descent: the Supporters are the Lion and the Unicorn, the heraldic emblems of the House of Judah and the House of Israel respectively; whilst on the Shield is the Harp of David. How is it possible to account for our possession of these heraldic emblems except on the supposition of our Israelitish origin.

Jacob's Stone—the Lia Phail, or Stone of Destiny.

According to tradition it was brought by one Brug (? Baruch, who always accompanied Jeremiah) from Egypt *via* Spain to Ireland, and kept at Tara, in Meath, where all the Irish monarchs were crowned. From thence it was taken, by Fergus, a brother of the Irish king who reigned at that time —Muisceortagh (Murkeetagh)—A.D. 513, in order that he might crown himself with greater solemnity King of Scotland; from which country it was ultimately brought by Edward I. to England, and by him placed in Westminster Abbey. It is known as Jacob's Stone, and upon it all our Kings and Queens have been crowned, except Queen Mary, who being a Roman Catholic, was crowned in a chair* blessed by the Pope.

The Kings of Israel during the time they dwelt in the land, on ceremonial occasions always "*stood by* (or *on*) the pillar (*ammud*) as the manner was" 2 Kings, 11. 14. May this not be the identical stone referred to? there is nothing improbable in the suggestion if it is borne in mind the watchful care that has been exercised over this relic for so many centuries in these Islands.

A very able Hebrew Scholar declares that the passage in Gen. 49, wherein Jacob's blessing of Joseph is recorded, might be rendered : " Hence-

---

* This chair is now preserved in Winchester Cathedral, as a curiosity.

forth he takes care of the stone of Israel," a prediction which has been thus literally fulfilled.

This Stone has for some 2400 years had the following prophetic Rune attached to it. Translated literally from the Irish Celtic according to the late Rev. F. R. A. Glover, M.A., it reads as follows:

> " The Wanderer's* Race, a noble Tribe,
> Unless Prophets false predict—
> Where they may find the stone of fate,
> Empire there, they've the right to assume."

Or, as it has been rendered by the late Sir Walter Scott,

> " Unless the fates have faithless grown,
> And prophet's voice be vain,
> Where 'er is found this sacred stone,
> The *Wanderer's* race shall reign."

The Kingdom of God.

If the British Nation is identical with the House of Israel it must also be the Kingdom of God in this world. The expression "Kingdom of God" is generally assumed to be synonymous with "the Kingdom of Heaven," and "Church of God." Whether that be so or not, one thing is very much apparent in the writings of Commentators and others, and that is, that the Kingdom of God is almost exclusively regarded in the so-called "spiritual" sense, to the utter disregard of the fact that there is and *must* be a literal Kingdom of God in existence on this earth at the present moment. This statement may appear startling to some

* Scuito; a Wanderer.—Celt. Dictionary.

people, but it is nevertheless true, as the following argument will prove.

Originally the Children of Israel were a theocracy. God was their King, therefore they were His Kingdom—the Kingdom of God. (2 Chron. 2. 1). The Chosen People murmured at this arrangement, with the result that God gave them a king in the person of Saul, who was succeeded by David, to whom it was promised that he should never want a man to sit on his throne for ever. David was succeeded by Solomon, and it is expressly stated in 1 Chron. 29. 23,

" Then Solomon sat on the throne of the Lord as king instead of David his father and prospered, and all Israel obeyed him."

Again, in 2 Chron. 9. 8,

" Blessed be the Lord thy God, which delighteth in thee, to set thee on His throne, to be king for the Lord thy God."

Solomon sat on a visible, material throne on this earth, ruling over the literal Kingdom of God, as represented by the Twelve-Tribed Nation. He occupied this position by virtue of the promise to David, as recorded in 2 Sam. 7, 12—16,

" When thy days be fulfilled, and thou shalt sleep with thy fathers, I will set up thy seed after thee, which shall proceed out of thy bowels, and I will establish his kingdom.

" He shall build an house for my name, and I will establish the throne of his kingdom for ever.

" I will be his father, and he shall be my son, if he commit iniquity, I will chasten him, . . .

"But my mercy shall not depart from him as I took it from Saul, whom I put away before thee.

"And thine house and thy kingdom shall be made sure for ever before thee: thy throne shall be established for ever."

It follows therefore, that wherever Israel exists as a nation (this cannot apply to the Jews, as they are a scattered people), there must be found the kingdom reigned over by a descendant of King David. Consequently, if our contention is correct (and we challenge proof to the contrary) that we are the Lost House of Israel, it follows beyond all dispute that our Nation is the Kingdom of God. Whilst contending for this great honor, with all its privileges and obligations for "to whomsoever much is given, of him shall be much required;" we desire to draw attention to the fact entirely lost sight of (if ever realized), that, wherever our Empire extends, there our Missionaries go and preach the Gospel of Christ, so that the Kingdom of God is thus both literally and spiritually extended at one and the same time.

Those who accept Christianity, be it remembered, become the sons of Abraham by adoption or faith only, and are not like British-Israel the Chosen People, the literal as well as spiritual descendants of Abraham. For we, as the nation of Israel are heir to both the temporal and spiritual blessings, but as members in Christ we are on a spiritual equality with all His followers who are included in that much misunderstood and much abused term,

The Church.

Where is it and what is it? In the highest sense in which this expression is understood, it embraces all true believers in Jesus Christ, of whatsoever Church or Denomination.

Matt. 21. 43, "The kingdom of God shall be taken away from you (Jews) and shall be given to a nation bringing forth the fruits thereof."

Commentators and others tell us that what is here called "a nation," really means "a Church." The result of not allowing the Bible to speak for itself is, that Sceptics and Freethinkers are led to declare: 'The Bible says one thing, and you say another, one or the other must be wrong; we decline to have anything to do with either.' On the other hand we find, whatever the professions of the Churches may be as a Christian Body, that when it comes to putting them into practice; the Roman Catholics claim that their's is the true Church and that all outside its pale are Schismatics: and that some members of the Church of England—as represented by an extreme section—say that there is "no salvation out of the Church," which assertion, carried to its logical conclusion, generally means their Church. The outcome of all this is, the sectarian strife, bitterness, and jealousy, which is such a disgrace to Christianity, and so disgusts many, that they either eschew religion altogether, becoming Sceptics or Freethinkers, or else relapse into utter indifference.

Taking the Bible as it stands, we find that the Kingdom of God was to be "given to *a nation* bringing forth the fruits thereof," and not to the

Gentiles in general, who are composed of many nations. "It is remarkable that Dean Alford commenting on this passage says: "*The Nation* here spoken of is not the Gentiles in general, but *the Church of the truly faithful, the 'holy nation,' 'peculiar people,' of Peter 2. 9, see Acts 15. 14.*" "The italics are his own, but these terms are applied by St. Peter himself as the context will show, to the Lo-Ammi, Ten-Tribed Israel of the Dispersion, as the Apostle's description of them, that they "*who in times past were not a people,*" cannot be applied to Gentile nations, far less to Gentile Churches." *

That nation therefore must be Israel, or Ephraim which is synonymous with Israel, and means "fruitful." It is stated in Isaiah 27. 6:

"In days to come shall Jacob take root: Israel shall blossom and bud: and they shall fill the face of the world with fruit,"—this we do both literally and spiritually, as a prosperous mercantile and missionary people.

May not the very object of the division of the twelve-tribed nation under Rehoboam have been, that Judah might witness for God in the Old, as we do for Him in the New, Dispensation. One may search the Bible from Genesis to Revelation, and to no one will it be found that the Oracles of God were committed, but Israel:

"O Children of Israel . . . you only have I known of all the families of the earth" (Amos 3. 1, 2).

"He sheweth His word unto Jacob, His statutes and His judgments unto Israel.

"He hath not dealt so with any nation:"

*Quoted by Dr. Grant in his "*Israel in the New Testament.*"

"And as for his judgments, they have not known them" (Psalm 147. 19—20).

It is to Israel—" a Nation," and not a "Church" as that word is generally understood,—that the the Oracles of God were to be intrusted.

To put this argument in another and perhaps more forcible or logical manner. Amongst Theologians and Commentators, the Olive Tree of Romans 11 is always regarded as symbolical of the Church, and is thus explained: "the root" is Abraham, "the branches" are the Twelve Tribes of Israel, whilst the "wild olive" is the Gentile Church. St. Paul says:

"And if the root is holy, so are the branches,

"But if some of the branches were broken off, and thou, being a wild olive, was grafted in among them, and didst become partaker with them of the root of the fatness of the olive tree;

"Glory not over the branches: but if thou gloriest, it is not thou that bearest the root, but the root thee. . . .

"Thou wilt say then, Branches were broken off, that I might be grafted in.

"Well; by their unbelief they were broken off, and thou standest by faith.

"Be not high minded, but fear: for if God spared not the natural branches, neither will he spare thee.

"Behold then the goodness and severity of God: towards them that fell, severity; but towards thee, God's goodness, if thou continue in his goodness: **otherwise thou shalt be cut off.**

"And they also, if they continue not in their unbelief, shall be grafted in: for God is able to graft them in again."

What became of the natural branches that were never broken off? They are not represented by the Jews; they could not possibly be by the Gentiles; therefore *they must be by Israel*—Israel of the "lost sheep of the House of Israel."

It does not follow that because the Gentile "wild olive graft" has been temporarily admitted into the Church of God, that therefore the *whole* became a Gentile Church. The simile is contrary to nature, as likewise to the actuallity, and the teaching of Holy Scripture.

Admission into the Church of God in the Mosaic Dispensation, was by the rite of circumcision, this has been superseded by the rite of baptism in this the Christian age.

In the Wilderness, the whole Congregation was the Church of God, *ergo*, the Nation was the Church. In England (the term is used in its widest sense), before Nonconformity was allowed, the National Church included the whole people; therefore, if the British people be literal Israel, the Nation was the Church, and the Church, as an Ecclesiastical Organization, was the Church of God in Great Britain, whilst Great Britain, as the Missionary Nation, is the Church of God in the world.

The various Non-Conformist Denominations, upon whose successful efforts, the blessing of God undoubtedly rests, may be fitly typified by the smaller branches, or out-growth from the main, natural branches, as represented by the English, Welsh,

Scotch, and Irish National Churches,—Home and Colonial.

The Roman Catholic Church, as a matter of fact, includes the purely Gentile Nations: nations which make no claim to be of literal Israelitish descent, whilst the British Protestant people, whether Churchmen or Nonconformists, claim that great honour. By virtue of that distinction, and the consequent continuity of the British Church from the Hebrew (not Jewish) Church in the Wilderness, our National Church is undoubtedly "the true Church."*

The pretensions of the Roman Church are thus effectually disposed of, and her arrogant assertions that the Anglican Orders are invalid, bear out her prophetical destiny of boasting against the natural branches, and should be treated with the calm and dignified contempt they deserve.

If the Clergy and Laity only realised the force of this argument, we should hear less about the age and continuity of the Church of Rome and become more fully alive to the glorious origin and destiny of our own. The cry of "Disendowment and Disestablishment" would not only sensibly diminish when the people realised the divine origin of our National Church, but would inevitably rally to its

* The Roman Mission of St. Augustine was not until A.D., 597, whereas Christianity was introduced into these Islands, prior to the destruction of Jerusalem by the Romans in A.D., 70, by Joseph of Arimathea, who fled from Palestine about A.D. 39, to this country, and built the first Church at the Isle of Avalon, now called Glastonbury, which was regarded as the most holy place in Britain for 1500 years after, and was free from taxation in consequence. There are also good reasons for believing that St. Paul preached Christianity in these Islands.

support many who are at present—no doubt from conscientious motives—opposed to a State Church.

What is really wanted by the vast mass of the people, is not Rome, but Home re-union.

Jew, Israelite, and Gentile.

It is generally assumed that Englishmen are a Gentile people in the sense in which that term is generally understood—*but they are not*. Judged by their writings, Theologians regard the two former terms as synonymous, whilst all who are not so included are described as Gentiles.

All Jews are Israelites but not all Israelites are Jews: just the same as all Hampshire men are Englishmen, but not all Englishmen are Hampshire men. It is not too much to say, that the inability to recognise this elementary but all-important definition, is the cause of all the confusion and misapplication of texts to the respective Houses of Israel and Judah. The result is simply lamentable, as it plainly nullifies the teaching of the Scriptures, and raises difficulties, where none need exist.

The term "Jew" was first given to the sons of Judah, the son of Israel, and afterwards applied to their descendents, who formed the House of Judah. The first mention of the word "Jew," is in 2 Kings 16. 6, which Book was written after the Babylonian captivity of the House of Judah. It is therefore absolutely erroneous and misleading to speak of the Jews in Egypt, the Jewish Law, &c., as such expressions exclude the Ten Tribes.

The Lost House of Israel were Israelites by virtue of their common descent from Israel, but they claimed no descent from Judah, or to the title of his House. With the divorcement of the Ten Tribes from the Mosaic Covenant, and their deportation to Assyria, where they were lost; the Jews became the sole representatives of Israel.

It must also be borne in mind that the distinction between an Israelite and a Gentile in the Old Testament Dispensation was simply this, that one was under the Mosaic Law, and the other was not. Hence, when Paul, who was a Benjaminite, called himself a Jew, this term was for the above reasons synonymous with Israel; by this explanation an apparent contradiction is reconciled, and a difficulty removed.

The term "Gentile" is equally and erroneously assumed to refer to all peoples and nations not of the elect line of Abraham's seed. Such an assumption is absolutely incorrect. There are Gentiles *and* Gentiles: one divison being Gentiles by faith but not by descent, as the lost House of Israel: the other purely Gentile, with no claim to literal descent, but who become the Children of Abraham by adoption or faith.

It is assumed that when St. Paul said to the Jews, "Lo, we turn to the Gentiles and they will hear us," he meant the heathen nations: on the contrary, it was the "Lo-Ammi" House of Israel to whom he referred. A very slight examination of

The New Testament proves the Conversion of the Lost Ten Tribes to Christianity, *
as demonstrated by the internal evidence of the Epistles to the so-called Gentile Churches.

* This argument is taken from a Pamphlet entitled *Israel in the New Testament*, by the late Surgeon-General Grant,

The Epistle to the Romans was addressed to "those who knew the law," which the Gentiles pure did not: "called to be saints,"—a title applied to Israel *only* throughout the Old Testament.

Corinthians—to those whose "fathers were all under the cloud, and all passed through the sea; and were all baptised unto Moses."

Galatians—who although redeemed from the law, were reproachfully asked:

"How turn ye back *again* to the weak and beggarly rudiments, whereunto ye desire to be in bondage over again.

"Ye observe days, and months, and seasons, and years."

Dean Alford says "the Galatians were Gentiles, not yet circumcised, although nearly persuaded to it by Judaising teachers," *ergo* they were not converted Jews.

It should be noted that Christ is the "Saviour" and not the "Redeemer" of the world. He came to redeem those who were under the Mosaic Law—a Law which never applied to Gentiles, but only to Israelites.

Ephesians—"And you did he quicken, when ye were dead through your trepasses and sins." This could not apply to the heathen, because "where there is no law, neither is there trangression," (Rom. 4. 15): also called the "*Uncircumcision*" by the Jews—a term which is never applied to the heathen nations indiscriminately. "Alienated from the commonwealth of Israel and strangers from the covenants of promise," with which the heathen world never had any concern.

Colossians—"And you, being in time past alienated . . . hath he reconciled in the body of his flesh through death," which implies previous covenant relationship to which the heathen were strangers.

The Hebrews—Christian Hebrews, therefore not Jews, as the latter not only refused to recognise Christ, but crucified Him.

It may be as well to point out, that it is not contended that all the people to whom the Epistles were addressed were exclusively " the lost sheep of the house of Israel;" but that primarily they were written for their instruction, as the above passages indicate. Further it must be borne in mind that St. Paul in particular, and the Disciples in general, were commissioned to " go not into the way of the Gentiles [pure], but go ye rather to the lost sheep of the House of Israel," who in turn, would preach the Gospel to the real Gentiles or heathen, amongst whom their lot was cast.

This commission therefore proves that wherever the Disciples went in obedience to our Lord's command, those to whom they preached were members of the House of Israel, consequently their whereabouts was not unknown to the followers of our Lord in those days.

The teaching of the Bible is that, whilst the acceptance of Christianity is open to all nations, the preaching of it is committed to God's chosen people Israel. Turning from prophecy to its fulfilment, it will be admitted that the people who make it their special duty to carry the Gospel to all nations, is pre-eminently the British Nation, which thus fulfils the *rôle* of Israel—"Ye are my witness that I am God."

The British Empire and the Stone Kingdom Identical.

The five great Empires of the world are universally admitted to be the Babylonian, Medo-Persian, Grecian, Roman, and last but not least, the British Empire. The Image seen by Nebuchadnezzar in his dream was explained by Daniel (chap. 2) as representing the political sequence of the kingdoms of this earth.

The kingdom of Babylon, was represented by "the head of gold."

The inferior kingdom of Medo-Persia, by "the breast and arms of silver."

The kingdom of Greece, by "the belly and thighs of brass," as the fighting men wore brazen armour: whilst

The Roman Empire, which was "part clay and part iron," was to become disintegrated and ultimately reappear in the form of "ten toes" or smaller kingdoms.

So far Commentators are agreed in the interpretation of this prophecy.

But when it comes to the question of declaring what is typified by the "Stone cut out of the mountain without hands," eventually to "fill the whole earth," and "a kingdom to be set up by the God of heaven in the days of those kings, which shall never be destroyed, nor shall the sovereignty thereof be left to another people, but it shall break in pieces and consume all these kingdoms, and it shall stand for ever:" they all with one consent proclaim, that this 'is the spiritual kingdom of Christ, which is to become universal by everyone accepting Christianity, and thereby owning allegiance to Christ, who will reign over His spiritual subjects in heaven as King.'

Now why, in the name of common sense and arguing from analogy, if all the other kingdoms were literal, why should not this, the "Stone" Empire be also literal? We contend that it is, and that just as the other Empires were symbolised by gold, silver, brass, and iron, so this, the greatest Empire the world has ever seen, is typified by a stone—Jacob's stone—in Westminster Abbey.

This Island of ours was "cut off without hands" from France by the erosion of the tide, which ebbs and flows twice in every twenty-four hours, and from here the British dominion has spread, and will continue to spread, all over the Globe, until the promise to Abraham, that his seed should become the "heir of the world," is fulfilled. Geologists admit that this Island was once joined to the mainland of France, but has been severed in the manner indicated.

It is evident that if we are not the "Stone" Kingdom, there is no reference to the British Empire in Daniel's forecast: for to suppose as some do, that the British Empire, which is five times as large as the Roman Dominions, is symbolised by a tenth part of it, as represented by one of the toes, is at once both absurd and illogical.

The Parables.

These seem to be generally regarded as having been written, like Æsop's Fables, merely for the purpose of moral instruction. Whilst not objecting that many useful and instructive lessons may in this manner be drawn from the Parables, there can be little doubt that their primary object was in the nature of a prophecy. They nearly all refer to the "kingdom of heaven." By way of illustration turn to the Parable of the Mustard Seed (Matt. 13. 31—32), "the kingdom of heaven is like unto a grain of mustard seed . . . which indeed is less than all seeds: but when it is grown, it is greater than the herbs, and becometh a tree, so that the birds of the heaven come and lodge in the branches thereof."

What is this but comparing it in another form to the kingdom of Israel, which originally was the smallest of all nations, but now as the kingdom of British-Israel has grown to be the greatest nation on earth, and under its protection all men of every kindred can and do dwell. This is in accordance with the prediction of Ezekiel (chap 17. 28), previously referred to in the transplanting of the "tender twig."

The Parable of the Rich Man and the Beggar named Lazarus, may be regarded as a prophecy of the downfall of Jerusalem and the escape of the Benjaminite Jews.

"A certain rich man, clothed in purple and fine linen, faring sumptuously every day"—the Jews and their manner of dress and living in those days, as also of the Levites, who fared sumptuously on the enormous tithes they then enjoyed.

"The beggar Lazarus, whom even the dogs came and licked his sores,"—"Jews" of the Tribe of Benjamin, who in accepting Christianity, were cast out by their brethren of Judah, and taken compassion on by the "dogs of Gentiles."

"The beggar was carried into *Abraham's bosom*"—a Jewish expression for Paradise—whilst Dives is in torments: this passage of course cannot be taken in the old-fashioned literal sense of "hell fire," as to put water on a man's tongue when in fire, would turn it into steam and add to his sufferings instead of alleviating them.

Dives says: "I have *five* brethren"—Leah had six sons, of whom Judah was one.

Abraham replies: "They have Moses and the prophets; let them hear them"—"If they hear not Moses and the prophets, neither will they be persuaded if one rose from the dead." Had the Jews properly studied the Scriptures, they would have known the manner of Christ's coming and have believed; but as it was, they were not even persuaded when Christ actually did rise from the dead.

"Beside all this, between us and you there is a great gulf fixed, that they which would pass from him to you may not be able, and that none may cross from them to us."—During the raising of the siege of Jerusalem, Eusebius tells of some Christian "Jews" escaping in obedience to a prophetic warning, and there can be little doubt that these Christians were none other than the Benjaminite Jews taking heed to the prophecy contained in Jer.

6. 1. When the Roman Army again closed round Jerusalem, escape was of course impossible; added to which the fearful sufferings these Jews underwent, fully bears out the description of being "in torment," whilst Benjamin was "afar off" in the mountains of Bethhaccharem, or "Paradise" compared to the position of their unfortunate brethren the Jews.

Attention is drawn to the fact, that whereas in the opening of the 16th chapter of St. Luke, verse 1, Christ spoke "unto His disciples," in verses 14, 15, Jesus speaks directly to the Pharisees themselves, and it is only after reciting this particular Parable that our Saviour again turns to the disciples, as seen on referring to the first verse of the following chapter.

Having given an outline of the theory that Englishmen are Israelites, it may be useful to give

A Resumé of the Argument.

Our Forefathers of the House of Israel have been traced from Samaria to the scene of their Captivity in the Cities of the Medes, South-west of the Caspain Sea; from thence to Arsareth in Moldavia, whence they passed through Germany, Norway, etc., into the British Isles, under the various names of Angles, Saxons, Jutes, Danes, and Normans, being now known collectively as the English or British people.

The British Isles have been identified as their predicted home in the Isles of the Sea, N.W. from Palestine.

The footsteps of Dan and Benjamin have also been specially traced in detail; and of Dan it may truly be said that he has maintained the custom of his tribe, in giving names to the places wherein he dwelt or passed through.

It is held that our Israelitish Ancestors passed through Germany unmixed with the various races inhabiting that and other countries, across which their journey lay, in the same manner by way of illustration the Gulf Stream flows through the Atlantic.

Parenthetically, attention may be drawn to the prediction that the resurrection and restoration of Lost Israel, is foretold by Ezekiel in his Vision of the Valley of Dry Bones.

"The bones came together, bone to his bone."—the various tribes assembling in these Islands.

"Come from the four winds, O spirit, and breathe upon these slain, that they may live,"—the spirit of Christianity.

"And the breath came into them and lived, and they stood up upon their feet, an exceeding great army."—a multitudinous people.

"Then he said unto me, Son of man, these bones are the whole house of Israel: behold, they say, Our bones are dried up, and our hope is lost; we are clean cut off."—from our brethren of Judah.

"Therefore prophesy, and say unto them, Thus saith the Lord God: Behold, I will open your graves, and cause you to come up out of your graves, O my people; and I will bring you unto the land of Israel."

"And ye shall know that I am the Lord, when I have opened your graves, and caused you to come up out of your graves, O my people."

It is evident from these words, that the Lost House of Israel buried in their "graves" and out of sight, are to stand forth as the people of God, after their return to Palestine in union with their brethren of Judah, as symbolised by joining of the "two sticks," and there exist as "one nation," "and one king shall be king to them all."

The various names under which the Ten Tribes were designated have been stated successively as, the House of Israel, Joseph, Ephraim, Isaac, or All Israel. They have also been identified as Beth Khumri—the House of Omri—the name given them by the Assyrian inscriptions: under the ethnic name of "Gimiri," the Semitic equivalent of the Aryan name Saka: and finally that the Gimiri of the Assyrian inscriptions are the Cimmerioi of the Greeks, the Cimbri of the Romans, and the Cymry of Wales.

The collective term "British" has been suggested as derived from two Hebrew words, "*B'rith*" and "*Ish*," Covenant Man,—Covenant People,—by virtue of our Abrahamic descent.

The similarity of the idiom of the British with the Hebrew tongue has also been pointed out.

The change of faith from the Mosaic to the Christian religion has been shown to be not so unaccountable as may at first sight appear, if the prophecies of Isaiah and Hosea are borne in mind.

The Birthright Blessings, by virtue of which the sons of Joseph, Ephraim and Manasseh, were respectively to become the head of "a nation and a company of nations," and a "great people"; have been explained as fulfilled in Great Britain and her Colonies, and the American people.

It must be borne in mind that these blessings were not fulfilled in the Mosaic Dispensation, they cannot be fulfilled in the Millennial Age,—because then both Israel and Judah are to be united as one nation on the mountains of Israel, no more to be rooted up—therefore they *must* be in course of realization in this the Christian Dispensation, to the House of Israel, or "the Scriptures are of no effect," which God forbid.

It has likewise been demonstrated :—

> That we are a multitudinous people.
> That we possess the gates of our enemies.
> That we dwell in safety—alone—in the appointed place in the Isles of the Sea.
> That this is a free country.
> That many are proud to surname themselves (Anglo) Israelites.
> That we are a mighty Empire, and a company of the nations.
> That to us is given the dominion of the sea.
> That we are under Divine protection.
> That we are the Missionary people of the earth.
> That we possess a magnificent heathen Empire in India.
> That we possess an invincible Army and Navy.
> That we are the great money-lending people.
> That we are a blessing to other nations, as the missionary and the great commercial people.

That we are a Sabbath-keeping people, both nationally and by law.

That we live under a Monarchy claiming descent from David.

That we possess a dual form of government known as Church and State.

That we rule over many nations.

That we put down slavery.

That we possess many customs of Hebrew origin, and finally

That the birthright blessings were to take effect in the "latter" days, or this the Christian Dispensation.

It may be asked, and as a matter of fact often is, Grant that the Anglo-Israel theory is correct, what is the good of it?

This of course is the old question of,

Cui Bono?

A little earnest consideration of, and reflection on, the arguments which have been adduced in support of this great truth, will bring home to the mind of the enquirer:

That it proves the inspiration of the Scriptures.

That it proves the faithfulness of God to His Promises made to our Forefathers Abraham, Isaac, and Jacob.

That it is the key to the interpretation of the Old Testament Prophets.

That it creates an intelligent and earnest interest in the study of the Bible, to the utter destruction of that scepticism and indifference which is so much deplored by the Clergy and Ministers of all denominations at the present time.

That it leads us to trust in God, in times of national and individual anxiety.

It proves the validity of our Anglican Orders.

It furnishes a conclusive answer to the erroneous claims and assertions of the Church of Rome; claims which are unsupported by Scripture, and historically are contrary to well-known facts.

It explains the source of many Hebrew customs and traditions which are extant amongst us.

It proves the brotherhood of the British and Jewish people, by virtue of their common Hebrew descent.

It therefore tends to prevent any jealousy or ill-feeling against the Jews, whenever and wherever, by virtue of their superior talents or industry, they rise to positions of influence in the Queen's dominions.

It is an effective argument in support of the claim that Missionary efforts have on our Nation for more extended and increased support.

It bids us also act up to our national responsibilities as the Chosen People, we being the ordained instruments of God in carrying out His purposes in this world.

It furnishes a reasonable and intelligent answer to the unbelief or doubts of the Atheist or Freethinker,

Finally, it calls for loyalty to Her Majesty the Queen, and *the* Royal Family, whose significant Motto, is
Dieu et mon Droit.

The Service of our National Church bears witness to this Great Truth,

if it is read and understood in a *literal* as well as spiritual manner, and gives the Service a force and meaning which those who blind to our Israelitish origin are strangers to, thereby depriving themselves of a benefit and pleasure which no one can realise until they have experienced it.

Had the Book of Common Prayer been specially framed to express the belief of Anglo-Israelites, no better words could have been chosen than those therein made use of. Such passages as the following,—out of many—all contain copyright terms applicable to Israel alone.

"We are thy people and the sheep of thy pasture."

"We have erred, and strayed from thy ways like lost sheep."

"O, Lord, save thy people. And bless thine inheritance."

"Give peace in our time, O Lord. Because there is none other that fighteth for us, but only thou, O Lord."

The "Benedictus" too, how full of meaning to those who realise their Israelitish origin.

Would that the Clergy, as well as the people, realised the beautiful impressiveness of our glorious Church Service, when thus taken in its literal meaning; surely to regard these Prayers and

Responses as so many now do, as merely having a spiritual meaning, applicable to every other Christian people, equally with our own, is to make them meaningless phrases.

———o———

This Anglo-Israel truth is one which should carry great weight with, and be of interest to, both Jews and Gentiles, as

Our Lord's Advent is proved by our Idenity with Israel.

It is well known that the Jews, with few exceptions, refuse to believe in our Saviour's first Advent.

The learned Dr. Neubauer, in a series of Articles contributed to the *Jewish Quarterly Review* in 1889, wrote as follows: "The return of the Ten Tribes was one of the great promises of the prophets, and the advent of the Messiah is therefore necessarily identified with the epoch of their redemption."

Now, if the arguments adduced are sufficiently convincing to them, that the British Nation is identical with the House of Israel, by the fact of being in possession of the promises and blessings made to Abraham, Isaac, and Jacob, and their descendants, the children of Israel; must it not only be proof positive that Christ has indeed come, but also account for the Lost Ten Tribes being under the New Covenant, by virtue of their redemption from the Mosaic law, under which they—the Jews—by rejecting Christ, still remain?

Missions to the Jews

are not likely to meet with much success in their efforts to convert them to Christianity, when the

Missionaries practically teach them that by changing their religion from the Mosaic to the Christian faith they become Gentiles. The Covenant People, like the Apostles in Christ's time, as evidenced by the latter's enquiry, "Lord wilt thou at this time restore the kingdom to Israel," are well aware that they are the inheritors of great temporal blessings. If, however, it was explained to them, that in accepting the Christian religion, they would be only following the example of their Brethren of the House of Israel, who in consequence of their acceptance of the New Covenant, came into possession of, and are thereby actually enjoying, those very promises the Jews themselves are expecting: would not one of the great obstacles to their acceptance of the Christian faith be removed? God grant that it may be so.

This same argument will likewise enable anyone to be

"Ready always to give answer to every man that asketh you a reason, concerning the hope that is in you."

It is only too probable that many people, whether Christians or Mohammedans, if asked why they believe in their respective religion, would be unable to give a better or more intelligent reply than, 'that they were brought up in that particular faith, and therefore they believe in it.' Doubtless they are sincere in their belief: but for good or ill, the day has gone by when men believe in religion, simply because the Clergy or their Parents tell them it is the right thing to do. A great many thinking men doubt, or refuse to believe, what they cannot understand. They want a plain answer to a plain question; not the dogmatic assertion, 'the Church teaches it, and therefore you must believe it.'

It is the absence of a convincing or satisfactory explanation of so many passages in the Scriptures, that causes that scepticism and indifference which is so marked a feature of the present generation. Is it to be wondered at, when all the glorious promises made to the House of Israel, instead of being shown to have a *literal* fulfilment, are explained away as having a *spiritual* application only, thereby "making them of none effect." One has only to turn to an Authorised Version of the Bible, to see that this statement is correct. The headlines explain the contents, as " Blessings to the Church," instead of to Israel, for whom they are really intended. It is a sincere cause for thankfulness that the Revised Version wisely omits the headlines altogether.

There are whole chapters in the Old Testament full of warning and comfort to us in the present time of national difficulty and anxiety, but for all the allusion that is ever made to them, they might as well have never been written. It is only the natural outcome after all, of that pernicious system of so called spiritual mode of interpretation, to the utter disregard of the literal application of the prophetical Scriptures, that they are not capable of explanation, by those to whom we have a right to look for instruction thereon.

Well might Isaiah declare:

"And all vision is become unto you as the the words of a book that is sealed, which men deliver unto one that is learned, saying, Read this, I pray thee: and he saith, I cannot for it is sealed.

"And the book is delivered to him that is not learned, saying, Read this, I pray thee: and he saith, I am not learned." (Chapter 29. 11—12).

A Suggestion to the Clergy

is respectfully offered. If besides preaching the Gospel, they would only show men of the world, and especially business men, by an intelligent exposition of the Old Testament Prophets, how much of their temporal anxiety might be relieved, if they realised that we as a nation have nothing to fear from our enemies abroad, in consequence of our being promised (Isaiah 54) the special protection of the Almighty God—as witness the Spanish Armada and the threatened Napoleonic invasion,—an interest would thereby be aroused in the Bible, which does not at present exist, and then men would come to Church for instruction, instead of remaining away, as so many at present do.

It is very hard, when everything seems to be going wrong, for men to be persuaded when they are admonished by the Clergy to,

Put your trust in God, and all will come right.

They have a vague idea that the advice is sound, the difficulty is to bring themselves to believe it; but bring home to their minds the conviction that our national experience has justified the advice, and a foundation is established for believing the admonition on personal grounds, as also for accepting those higher mysteries of the Christian Religion, which appeal more to faith than reason.

Elaborate ceremonies, and ornate ritual are all very well in their way, but men who have to put up with the rough and tumble of this life, are seldom attracted by such means—most of them positively dislike it—as they are quick enough to perceive that extreme ritual, or its complete absence, will neither get them into heaven or keep them out of it.

Hints for Interpertation of the Scriptures.

The following suggestions may prove useful in the study of the Scriptures, by enabling the reader to ascertain to which House any particular passage may apply, and thus more readily help to elucidate its meaning.

1. There are three Dispensations—the Mosaic, the Christian, and the Millennial—included in the Bible. These are capable of further sub-division, such as the Patriarchal, Mosaic ages, &c., but it is not necessary to go into such comparatively minute details for the purpose in view.

2. Bear in mind the dates inserted in the margin of the (A.V.) Bible: also that the House of Israel was finally carried captive in B.C. 721, and ceased to be a people in B.C. 677 (Isaiah 7. 8, 9). Further remember,

3. That there are distinctive terms under which the two Houses of Israel are mentioned, both in the Old, as well as the New Testament.

Taking these suggestions in the order given, they will be perhaps better comprehended if each is accompanied by an explanation of some passage from the Scriptures, in order to illustrate the foregoing directions.

1. Gen. 49. 10: "The sceptre shall not depart from Judah . . . Until Shiloh come."

The first verse of this chapter states, that this prophecy was to be fulfilled in the "latter days:" therefore it cannot apply to the Mosaic, but to the Christian Dispensation. The manner of its accomplishment, and the argument in support thereof, has been already stated on pages 56 and 65.

2. The Book of Obadiah: which dates about B.C. 587. The first half has already had one fulfilment during the Mosaic age at the time of the Babylonian Captivity, but whilst agreeing with those who believe it will have a secondary or complete accomplishment; the latter portion of this Book has never been fulfilled, for the following reason:—At the time Obadiah began to prophesy, the Ten Tribes, or "the House of Joseph" as they are called in verse 18, had been carried captive to Assyria some 130 years before, from which captivity they never returned; consequently, the event herein predicted must take place in the "latter days," because in the Millenial Dispensation, the two Houses of Israel and Judah will then be united as one nation for ever. This inference is confirmed by a reference to Numb. 24. 15—19, which alludes to the same incident.

3. Apart from their titular or national designation, such as the House of Judah, and House of Israel, Jacob, or Joseph, &c., the two Nations in the Old Testament are spoken of by certain fixed

terms of reproach :—"*backsliding*" Israel, as distinguished from "*treacherous*" Judah (Jer. 3. 8); "the *outcasts* of Israel, the *dispersed* of Judah" (Isaiah 11. 12). The Jews are also termed "the *rebellious* children" (Isaiah 30. 1): the marginal date opposite the last reference is B.C. 713, or nearly ten years after Israel was carried captive to Assyria: this fact, taken in conjunction with the context, which tells of their going "down to Egypt," is a proof that it refers to the Jews, and not to the House of Israel. Ezek. 3. 7—9, likewise speaks of the *rebellious* House of Judah: he prophesied B.C. 595 circ., at a time when the Ten Tribes had long been cut off from the Mosaic Covenant, and lost both their country, and covenant name of Israel.

In Isaiah 65, the condition of the two people is contrasted in both Dispensations. Verse 1, refers to Israel, but verses 2—7 apply to the Jews; whilst verses 8—12 refer to the future occupation by the House of Israel of the land of their inheritance. In the succeeding passages, 13—15 we find another means of distinguishing the two Houses, by the distinctive use of the pronouns "my" and "ye;" whilst the additional and honourable distinction of "servants," is the title, therein applied to British-Israel: "Behold, my servants shall eat, but ye shall be hungry," &c.

In the New Testament there is not the same difficulty which Nation to apply the term Israel, because, with very few exceptions, the passages always refer to the Jews, they being the sole outwardly known representatives of the Chosen People, owing to the disappearance many centuries before, of the Lost Ten Tribes, in accordance with the prophecies of the Old Testament Prophets, notably of Hosea.

The difficulty lies rather in distinguishing between the two classes of Gentiles referred to. Some as previously explained, were those " who desire to be in bondage over *again*" (to the Mosaic law), from which they had been "redeemed." Manifestly, this cannot refer to the Jews they having refused as a nation, to accept Christianity: neither can it be applied to Gentiles, their fathers not having been under the Levitical law: therefore, it must apply to " Lo-Ammi" outcast Israel of the Ten Tribes. St. Peter, in the first Epistle (chaps. 1 and 2), confirms this by quoting passages from Hosea which refer exclusively to the House of Israel, as distinguished from Judah.

The term "Saints" is alone applicable to the Chosen People,

and is only so applied in the Old Testament; this distinction is also perpetuated in the New Testament, the Gentiles pure being included in "the church" or else spoken of as "the faithful," *vide* the Epistles which are addressed to,

The "*saints* with all that call upon the name of our Lord Jesus Christ in every place *their* Lord and *ours*" (1 Cor. 1. 1—2):

" Unto the Church of God which is *at* Corinth, *with* all the *saints*." (2 Cor. 1. 1).

"To the *saints* which are *at* Ephesus, *and the faithful* in Christ Jesus." (Chapter 1. 1).

" To the *saints and faithful brethren* in Christ which are *at* Colossæ." (Chapter 1. 2).

"Peter, an apostle of Jesus Christ to *the elect* who are sojourners of the Dispersion," &c.

Election and Predestination

is also applicable only to literal Israel. St. Paul in his Epistle to the Romans (chap. 8), refers to the Lost House of Israel of whom, by accepting Christianity the Apostle says "there is therefore now no condemnation" (ver. 1): this is in contrast to their brethren the Jews, who prefer to remain under the Mosaic law, therefore "they that are in the flesh cannot please God" (ver. 9). St. Paul further declares of lost Israel (ver. 29—33, A.V.):

"For whom he did foreknew, he also did predestinate . . .

"Moreover whom he did predestinate, them he also called: and whom he called, them he also justified: and whom he justified, them he also glorified. . . .

"Who shall lay anything to the charge of God's elect? It is God that justifieth."

A declaration literally applied to Ten-Tribed Israel in Isa. 54. 17. Election and predestination, therefore, are terms of literal application to an elect people and a chosen generation, in the direct line of descent from Abraham, Isaac and Jacob, and not in the narrow sense so usually received: a select few of what is termed "very religious people," who generally appropriate this privilege to themselves to the exclusion of everyone else.

A Word of Warning and Explanation

may be necessary to prevent misunderstanding or

giving offence. Objections are sometimes raised, against advocates of Anglo-Israel theory :

That they are too prone to dwell exclusively on the literal aspect of this question, to the exclusion of the spiritual teaching inculcated in the Scriptures.

That the acceptance or study of this great truth, has a tendency to minister to a feeling of national pride and boastfulness, instead of that spirit of humility which becometh the servants of Christ.

That it is an eminently selfish argument, inasmuch as it is an attempt to claim the monoply of the Abrahamic blessings, both literal and spiritual, to the exclusion of other nations and peoples.

Finally; that literal blessings are made of more vital consequence than spiritual welfare, and descent from Abraham, is substituted for salvation through Jesus Christ alone.

Were one of these charges true, it would be sufficient to condemn the subject in the estimation of all Godfearing men : a little consideration and explanation will, however, show that they are made under a misapprehension, and without due regard to the facts of the argument.

The primary object of all advocates of this great truth and discovery of the end of the age, is, and must of necessity be, to show by fair argument and literal interpretation that Lost Israel is found in the British Nation.

The fact that the literal blessings promised by God on oath, to Abraham and his seed for ever, are fulfilled in us as a nation, as proved by the evidence of our being in actual enjoyment of them : is a practical justification of the claim, and a standing proof, in these days of scepticism and freethought, that God is not slack concerning His promises.

The Pulpit often points to God's dealings with the Jews, as an evidence of the truth of His word; but it unfortunately ignores this the greatest proof of all, and one too, that would come home with peculiar force to the very people it particularly concerns.

Surely if the literal application is considered conducive to spiritual edification in the one case, why not in the other?

Could the Clergy enforce spiritual lessons on their flock, if they always preached on temporal subjects? It is obviously impossible. How then is the importance of the literal interpretation of the Scriptures to be impressed if this argument was supported almost exclusively on the lines of spiritual explanation of the Old Testament prophecies. Would not the very object in view be defeated?

All Englishmen are proud of their nationality, and deservedly so: but is it not a still greater honour to be one of God's Chosen People? If the honour is great, the responsibility is undoubtedly greater, for "to whomsoever much is given, of him shall much be required." It is well for objectors to remember sometimes that there is "a pride that apes humility."

So far from being a selfish argument, it is quite the contrary. Its general acceptance would lead the nation to a higher sense of its responsibilities, and make the people realise in a way they have never done before that the literal blessings they enjoy, are not given to them for their own selfish possession, but that "the stranger that sojourneth with you shall be unto you as the homeborn among you." This, indeed, has always been the most marked characteristic of our "free country," and still more so since the adoption of Free Trade.

The charge that Abrahamic descent is substituted for salvation through Christ is baseless, as neither from the writings or speeches of any exponents of the theory can such charges be substantiated. It is in vain for anyone to rely for salvation on the fact that "we have Abraham to our Father:" for in Christ "and in none other is there salvation: for neither is there any other name under heaven, that is given among men, wherein we must be saved," but Christ only.

Few Men read the Old Testament.

They have a vague idea that it is either a history of the Jews, or else that it contains prophecies which, so far as they are intelligible, refer only to those people, and are consequently of no practical interest to anyone else. This result is the outcome of the present mode of spiritual, to the utter neglect of literal, interpretation, whereby the Old Testament Writings are so much Greek, for all the information that ordinary individuals can glean from them. The Bible has thus become a closed and neglected book, instead of a most interesting, edifying and instructive study, gradually leading men on to a belief and trust in a beneficent Creator.

Commentators and Theologians should carry out the Rule they themselves lay down.

viz: "that where the literal rendering will hold good it is to have the preference of the spiritual interpretation." If the Clergy would consistantly follow out this rule in their study of the Bible, in the new light of British Israel Truth, it is not too much to say, that nearly all their theological difficulties would disappear. Surely a subject which leads men to study the Bible, and enables them to realise the intense love of God for His People, in showering down as He undoubtedly has done, upon our unworthy nation, the greatest blessings both literal and spiritual, that any Empire in this world has ever received; is more worthy of consideration and a respectful hearing, than the contempt and abuse it too often meets with.

The Clergy must of necessity experience much difficulty in accepting this Theory.

It is difficult for them, no doubt, as it is for business men, to unlearn what they have learnt. They apparently have been taught by their Theological studies—judged by their sermons and writings, which teem with such misleading and incorrect phrases as, "The Jews in Egypt," "The Jewish Church in the Wilderness," "The Jewish Law," etc., thereby utterly ignoring the existence of the other *Hebrews*, the Ten Tribes—that the Jews are the sole representatives of Israel. All the prophecies therefore that will not apply to the Jews, are consequently applied to "The Church," *i.e.*, the General Body of Believers. To be told now that this a wrong application of the prophecies, and further that they are applicable to none other than to the British people, instead of as is conjectured by some the Afghans, Nestorians, or Red Indians, is a "large order," and more perhaps than they can be expected to swallow all at one dose. The objection too, is sometimes not diminished when the Anglo-Israel theory is propounded in some instances by individuals, who, in their estimation, may be perhaps deficient in education, social position, or possessed only of a smattering of theology. It is not to be forgotten, however, that the same remarks applied with equal force to the Apostles, who were nearly all men of humble position in life. It is only natural the Clergy should believe that they know their own business better than others who have not been trained to it, and some allowance must therefore be made for their inability, in too many instances it is to be regretfully admitted, to accept the views herein advocated.

It is however hoped, that in future, none will be deterred from studying this subject, by the imperfect or unhappily expressed writings or speeches of its various exponents, but rather that they may be led to share in the joyful conviction of the Writer, who, in the words of St. Paul, rejoices to be able to say with a spirit of true thankfulness to God:

"Are they Hebrews? So am I.

Are they Israelities? So am I.

Are they the seed of Abraham? So am I."

TURKS EDOMITES.

POLITICS and PROPHECY.

A Revised and Enlarged Reprint from
"The Covenant People," with Colored Map.

BY

H. HERBERT PAIN.

A Founder & Member of the Council of the British Israel Association.

(*Metropolitan, Provincial & Colonial.*)

TURKS EDOMITES,

Politics and Prophecy.

AMONGST the numerous suggestions put forward for the settlement of the Turkish Problem, all mention of the prophetical solution of this difficult question is conspicious by its absence.

It is obvious that before the second and final Return of the Chosen People to Palestine can take place, the present possessors of the Holy Land must cease to retain control of Israel's Inheritance.

That Turkey will give up without a struggle the posessssion of the Holy Places which have been under her dominion for so many centuries, is hardly to be expected. The end, however, of the Ottoman Empire is admittedly close at hand, but the means by which this much desired and long expected consummation will be brought about, is a matter of much political controversy at the present time.

The Old Testament Prophets declare with no uncertain voice, that God "will lay vengeance upon Edom by the hand of my people Israel," and that Palestine, Egypt, the Soudan, parts of Africa and Asia Minor, as well as at a later period Abyssinia, will become the possessions of the Chosen People.

There are prophetical reasons for believing that this will be brought about by the instrumentality of the British and American nations.

To understand the basis on which these expectations are founded, it is necessary to prove—

1 That the British and American people are identical with the House of Joseph.

2 The connection of the Ottoman Turks, with the House of Esau or Edom.

The argument in favour of the first proposition has already been explained in the previous portion of this Pamphlet, under the article entitled *Englishmen Israelites*, it therefore remains to prove on scriptural grounds the identity of Edom with Turkey.

In Genesis 36, it is declared that,

"Esau is Edom."

and his country—which in the time of Moses extended right up to the River Euphrates—is described as Mount Seir.

Bozrah was the metropolis, being identical in name with Basra or Bussorah near Bagdad, and Broussa in Asia Minor. The name means, "The Strong City."

Two of Esau's Grandchildren were Teman* and Omar, the latter name having been borne by the Caliph who built the famous Mosque at Jerusalem, the former (several times employed synonymously

---

* Teman or Theman, Hebrew תימן ת, the initial letter being generally rendered Th, as T has its own sound ט Thus the sound of the name in Hebrew is very nearly "Othman." But Othman himself, as Gibbon shows, was called Athman or Thaman. He gave its name to the dynasty of the Osmanli or Ottoman Turks. Latham, *Russian and Turk*; Oxonian, *Russia Japhet*, p. 114.

with Edom) being identical with Othman, Ottoman or Osmanli.

These are interesting corroborations of the conclusion drawn from a study of the Old Testament prophecies which represent Edom as the power in possession of Israel's land for centuries prior to Israel's now imminent restoration. The Turks are in possession. Therefore, the Turks are Edom.

"By thy sword shalt thou live" (Gen. 27. 40), is as true of his descendants to-day, as it was when Esau was blessed by his father Isaac: witness the "abomination of desolation" spread over some of the fairest portions of God's earth included in the Asiatic dominions of the Ottoman Empire.

It is also remarkable that the Sultan on ascending the Throne is "girt with a sword"—not crowned.

Ezekiel's Prophecy of Edom.

"Because thou hast said, These two nations and these two countries shall be mine, and we will possess it," Chap. 35. 10: *i.e.*, Judah and Israel—Judæa and Samaria. Also:

"The ancient high places are ours in possession" (Chap. 36. 2):

There can be no question that these predictions have already had a partial fulfilment at the close of the Mosaic Dispensation; but prophecy like history, often repeats itself, and those students of the prophetical Scriptures are doubtless correct, who hold that these predictions have a double, or future fulfilment. In this case there are numerous passages which can be quoted in support of that contention,

Ezekiel, foretelling the Restoration of the Chosen People, declares that at that time the people who are in possession of the land, is none other than Edom. His words are as follows:

"Surely in the fire of my jealousy have I spoken against the residue of the nations, and against all Edom, which have appointed my land unto themselves for a possession with the joy of all their heart, with despite of soul, to cast it out for a prey" (chap. 36).

Clearly the people who have for centuries past held, and at the present time hold Palestine, are the Ottoman Turks.

The Parable of Balaam. *

This prediction contained in Numbers 23. and 24, it must be remembered was delivered some 4,000 years ago, when Israel existed as a Theocracy, and dwelt in Palestine. The Prophet therefore, when called upon by Balak to curse Israel, saw the Chosen People in the far distant future, in their home of the "Isles of the West," "afar off," where they should live under a Monarchy claiming Davidic descent. Read in this light, his words which are as follows, are easily understood.

"How shall I curse, whom God hath not cursed?
And how shall I defy, whom God hath not defied?
For from the top of the rocks I see him:
Lo, it is a people that dwell alone,

---

* Balaam himself was a son of a King of Edom. Compare Joshua 13. 22, with 1 Chronicles 1. 43.

And shall not be reckoned among the nations.
Who can count the dust of Jacob,
Or number the fourth part of Israel?
Let me die the death of the righteous,
And let my *last end* be like his!"

"The Lord his God is with him,
And the shout of a king is among them.
He hath as it were the horns of the wild-ox
Behold, the people riseth up as a lioness,
And as a lion doth he lift himself up:
He shall not lie down until he eat of the prey,
And drink the blood of the slain."

"And his seed shall be in many waters,
And his king shall be higher than Agag, *
And his kingdom shall be exalted."

"Blessed be everyone that blesseth thee
And cursed be every one that curseth thee."

The Prophet then tells Balak:

"Come and I will advertise thee what this people shall do to thy people—and Edom—in the "*latter days*," a proof that these peoples were to have a separate national existence in this, the Christian Dispensation.

"And he took up his parable and said,

"I see him, but not now:
I behold him, but not nigh:
There shall come forth a star out of Jacob,
And a sceptre shall rise out of Israel.
And shall smite through the corners of Moab,
And break down all the sons of tumult
And Edom shall be a possession,

* In the LXX. "Agag" is rendered "Gog," *i.e.*, Russia.

Seir also shall be a possession, which were his
   enemies ;
While Israel doeth valiantly.
And out of Jacob shall one have dominion,
And shall destroy the remnant from the city."

May not this be the city of Psalm 60. 9—12 ?

"Who will bring me into the strong city ?
Who will lead me into Edom ?
Wilt not thou, O God, which *hast* cast us off ?*
   and goest not forth, O God, with our hosts ?
Give us help against the adversary :
For vain is the help of man.
Through God shall we do valiantly ;
For He it is that shall tread down our
   adversaries."

Granted that Edom is Turkey, their "strong city" now, without the shadow of a doubt, is Constantinople.

It is also evident from these declarations that when the moment for action arrives, British-Israel must enter Constantinople, solely relying on her own strong arms, and the help of God " for vain is the help of man."—*the isolation* of England !

Turn now to

The Vision of the Prophet Obadiah,

who prophesied exclusively of Edom and the House of Joseph : his declarations have a remarkable and most forcible application to the present political situation.

Obadiah dates from about B.C. 587, nearly 150 years after the Ten Tribes were exiled from their

---

* An allusion to the Assyrian Captivity of B.C. 710-721.

land, and where they were never known by the Prophet's designation. The reference, therefore, must of necessity have a future application, and that too, to the Christian dispensation, as in the Millenial age, the two Houses of Israel become no more two nations, but one.

"The vision of Obadiah.

"Thus saith the Lord God concerning Edom: We have heard tidings from the Lord, and an ambassador is sent among the nations, saying Arise ye, and let us rise up against her in battle."

This may refer to the mission of General Ignatieff, who was sent by Russia before the war of 1877, and it is also applicable now to the British Ambassador at Constantinople, who has long vainly endeavoured to persuade the Representatives of the Great Powers to unite in compelling the Sultan to ameliorate the condition of his Armenian and other oppressed subjects.

"Behold I have made thee small among the nations: thou art greatly despised."

This is undoubtedly true of Turkey at the present time.

The Prophet then goes on to declare, that Edom trusting to the security of his position will persist with fatal determination unto the end, in his defiant attitude. This correctly describes the position of Turkey to-day.

"All the men of thy confederacy have driven thee out, even to the border."

One by one the Provinces of Roumania, Montenegro, Servia, Bulgaria, &c., have struggled for and obtained their independence, until at the present time there is hardly anything left of the former vast possessions of the Sultan on this side of the Bosphorus. Turkey is literally "driven out even unto the border."

"The men that were at peace with thee have deceived thee, and prevailed against thee." Is this Russia?

"Shall I not in that day, saith the Lord, destroy the wise men out of Edom, and understanding out of the mount of Esau?"

Lord Salisbury, on the death of Rustem Pasha, deplored the loss to the Turkish Empire of such an able man, as he was, and said "that if the Sultan had more advisers of the same stamp about him, Turkey would not be going to its end in the way it is surely doing."

Finally, after enumerating the sins of Edom in past ages towards our brethren the Jews, Obadiah declares;

"For the day of the Lord is near upon all the nations: as thou has done, it shall be done unto thee; thy dealing shall return upon thine own head.

"And the house of Jacob shall be a fire, and the house of Joseph a flame, and the house of Esau for stubble, and they shall burn among them, and devour them: and there shall not be any remaining to the house of Esau; for the Lord hath spoken it."

It has been explained in the previous portion of this Pamphlet, that Ephraim is represented by England and her Colonies, and that Manasseh is represented by America: from the fact that they are here collectively referred to under the one head o their father's name, as the House of Joseph, it seems a fair inference that the two nations who are to inflict God's "vengeance upon Edom," are the English and American people.

What will bring about our joint Interference in the Affairs of Turkey,

it is difficult to forecast, but it is increasingly manifest that there is an intense feeling of indignation in this country, almost beyond words to express, at the massacres and nameless atrocities committed on the unfortunate Armenian subjects of the Sultan. That the renewal of these massacres in Constantinople and elsewhere is exciting the anger of all the British people almost beyond the limits of endurance, is evidenced by the public indignation Meetings which are being held all over the kingdom to protest in the name of Christianity, against the diabolical conduct of His Satanic Majesty, the Sultan of Turkey, and calling for his deposition by England, either with or without the assistance of the Great Powers.

The Great Obstacle

to enforcing such an extreme measure is the mutual distrust and jealousy of the European Nations (Isaiah 42, 13), or the fear that the active interference of England alone might provoke, as it certainly would do in most people's opinion, a general European War, thereby creating greater evils than those it is now sought to remedy. The knowledge that there are no less than 23,000,000 men all equipped with the most deadly weapons of warfare, and ready to fly to arms at the mere word of command of one of their Rulers, is enough to make any man pause before seeking the arbitrament of war, with all its nameless horrors: a war too that will be the most terrible the world has ever witnessed.

In spite of all diplomatic protests, the massacres and ill treatment of the Armenians and others continue, and the European Powers look on, seemingly helpless to prevent it. Everyone is asking his neighbour—What will be the outcome of it all?

In the light of the prophetical passages quoted, there is but one answer :—

England and America alone,

will bring about the deposition of the Sultan. For does not Ezekiel declare, " I will lay my vengeance upon Edom, by the hand of my people Israel": Balaam, that Israel is to "destroy the remnant from the city": the Psalmist, that Israel will appeal to God for "help against the adversary, for vain is the help of man": and finally Obadiah, that the House of Joseph shall devour the House of Esau"? Grant the argument is proved, that this nation is Israel, and Edom is identical with Turkey, then the solution of the Turkish Problem is thus clearly declared by the Old Testament Prophets.

But how?

It is obvious that to carry out our destiny of entering into "the strong city"—Constantinople—England and America could only attain that object by sending their united fleets up the Dardanelles, neither country being in a position to undertake a military expedition with the slightest hope of success.

Some people may object that only "feather headed firebrands" could entertain such an insane idea, that it is possible for the Fleets to survive such an ordeal as the forcing of the Dardanelles, which are so strongly fortified, as to be almost impregnable. Such objectors lose sight of the fact, that Providence has always specially protected this nation, as past incidents in the history of our country, have again and again proved.

"No weapon that is formed against thee shall prosper," will prove as true in the future national experience of British-Israel, as it has in the past.

Another great massacre, or rising of the Armenians might easily give rise to the same situation that existed at the time of the bombardment of Alexandria in 1882. Then the British Admiral gave notice to the Commanders of the various Foreign Fleets of his intention to carry out the orders of his Government, and inviting their co-operation, with the well-known result that they all backed out of the situation at the critical moment of action.

There seems every reason to anticipate that the mutual fears and jealousies of the Great Powers may have the same effect in the near future, but perhaps with far more serious consequences, for they may even combine to prevent this country from carrying out its declared intention.

Such a critical moment in our national career, would—judging from the speeches made in Congress, at the time of the last scare created by the

German Emperor's now historical telegram to President Kruger,—inevitably have the effect of uniting our American Brethren with the Old Country and the Colonies, in the hour of trial, against, may be, the threatened, but probably after all, passive opposition of the combined forces of Europe.

"And thy mighty men, O Teman, shall be dismayed," will then be the position of Turkey at that time in very truth.

Then will go up the prayer of the Psalmist, from the nation of British-Israel: "give us help against the adversary, for vain is the help of man."

The presence of the American Fleet in the Mediterranean, cruising off Smyrna, is ominously significant, as is also the objection of Russia, to Turkey permitting an American War Vessel to pass through the Dardanelles, in order to act as guardship to the Legation at Constantinople.

Some people may object to our interfering alone in the affairs of Turkey, on the plea urged by the venerable Mr. Gladstone, that "we have not had the sword of the Almighty entrusted to our keeping," but grant this nation is Israel, there cannot be the slightest doubt that to us apply the words of Jeremiah:

"Thou art my battle axe and weapons of war: and with thee will I break in pieces the nations, and with thee will I destroy kingdoms" (chap. 51. 20.)

Nor need we fear the result, for if God be with us, who can be against us?

It must also be remembered, that upon us, as

the Chosen People is laid the Divine command :

"To loose the bands of wickedness, to undo the bands of the yoke, and to let the oppressed go free, and that ye break every yoke.

"Is it not to deal thy bread to the hungry, and that thou bring the poor that are cast out to thy house? when thou seest the naked that thou cover him : and that thou hide not thyself from thine own flesh?" (Isaiah 58, 6—7.)

Once the Nation is roused to action, as indeed it bids fair soon to be,

Woe betide the unspeakable Turk.

Hear the words of the Prophet Isaiah (chap. 34), "For the Lord hath indignation against all the nations, and fury against all their host: he hath utterly destroyed them, he hath delivered them to the slaughter.

"For my sword hath drunk its fill in heaven; behold it shall come down upon Edom, and upon the people of my curse, to judgment."

"For the Lord hath a sacrifice in Bozrah, and a great slaughter in the land of Edom."

"And the *unicorns* (in A.V.) shall come down with them, and the *bullocks* with the *bulls* (the Colonies with England and America) and their land shall be soaked with blood, and their dust made fat with fatness."

"For it is the day of the Lord's vengeance, the year of recompense in the controversy of Zion."

England having accomplished her object in deposing the Sultan, may withdraw the Fleets in order to demonstrate to Europe the unselfishness of her motive, in putting an end to the intolerable state of affairs in the Turkish capital. There is, however, only too much reason to fear that active interference on our part will probably be the signal for the rising of all the oppressed races living under the iniquitous rule of the Sultan.

Macedonians, Greeks, Cretans, Armenians, Arabians, and Syrians will, there is only too much reason to believe, rise against their oppressors to a man, massacreing the Turks right and left, and small sympathy will the latter get from the rest of the world.

"As thou hast done, it shall be done unto thee" is the doom pronounced by Obadiah, and soon will it be realised.

It may be interesting to here draw attention to the recent significant letters of a Correspondent of *The Daily Graphic*, written in conversational form, on

"The Gangrene of Europe,"

inter alia, it was pointed out that :

"Out of earshot of the Turkish Officials pious Moslems whisper of the fate in store for Islam, and tell one another that the time draws nigh. There is a *Hadith* of the Prophet—a traditional teaching, you know—which says, 'There is no other Mahdi than Jesus, the Son of Mary,' and a gloss on this teaching declares that after the overthrow of the Turks in Europe, Jesus will descend on one of the minarets of the Grand Mosque at Damascus, and that then the Christians will enter the enclosure of the Mosque of Omar through the Gate Beautiful—the Golden Gate, which is now blocked up. Of late many devout Moslems have spoken to me of this tradition as pointing the inevitable way out of the present crisis. It is their picturesque way of anticipating a probable partition of Turkey among the Powers of Europe."

In conclusion the writer adds,

"In Jerusalem, for example, there is a great movement on foot just now to learn English. People tell you they are preparing for coming events—that in the impending convulsions the British will come out at the top; and they argue in this way: Russia and France, represented respectively by the Greek and Latin Churches, are, they say, irreconcileable.

That is quite true. You may talk of your Franco-Russian alliance in Europe, but in Asia Minor it does not, and never will, exist. Well, when Russia and France fall out, England will walk in. That is how the Syrian argues it out to himself, and he is not a very unsophisticated person."

Our Saviour's Prediction

in answer to the enquiry of the Disciples, as to the "signs of the end," seems in one passage to pointedly refer to this dreaded catastrophe; the violent destruction of Edom's Empire.

"Wheresoever the carcase is, there will the eagles be gathered together."

May not "the carcase" represent Turkey, and "the eagles" the heraldic emblems of all the Great Powers, who are preparing to scramble for "the sick man's inheritance," thereby becoming involved in a

General European War from which England will be Exempted,

if our expectations are realised.

The reasons for this anticipation are based on the interpretation of the 26th Chapter of Isaiah, a chapter which deals with events leading up to the occupation of "the land of Judah" by British-Israel.

"Open ye the gates, that the righteous nation which keepeth truth may enter in."

"Thou wilt keep him in perfect peace, whose mind is stayed on thee: because he trusteth in thee."

"Lord thou wilt ordain peace for us."

"Thou hast increased the nation, O Lord, thou hast increased the nation; thou art glorified: thou hast enlarged all the borders of the land."

"Come my people, enter thou into thy chambers, and shut thy doors about thee: hide thyself for a little moment, until the indignation be overpast.*

"For, behold, the Lord cometh out of his place to punish the inhabitants of the earth for their iniquity: the earth also shall disclose her blood, and shall no more cover her slain."

In view of the argument contained in these pages, and the above passages, call to mind the declaration of Isaiah (54. 17), that "their righteousness which is of me, saith the Lord," is applied to the House of Israel † not Judah: also how England for some years past, has been fortifying her Home and Colonial Defences, and strengthening her Army and Navy, in view of her isolation, and the jealousy of the Foreign Powers, with any of whom, each successive Government of the Queen, both Conservative and Liberal, has consistently refused to enter into alliance.

The nation's borders have been truly enlarged, especially during the reign of Her Most Gracious Majesty the Queen, and bid fair to be still further

---

* The preceding verse (19): "Thy dead men shall live; my dead bodies shall arise. Awake and sing, ye that dwell in the dust: for thy dew is as the dew of herbs, and the earth shall cast forth the dead," does *not* refer to the final day of resurrection at the end of the world, but to the spiritual resurrection of the dry bones of the House of Israel, as depicted in Ezekiel. A reference to John 5. 25 proves this: "Verily, verily, I say unto you, the hour is coming, *and now is*, when the dead shall hear the voice of the Son of God, and they that hear shall live." This is different from the resurrection of the dead "from the tombs," when "the hour cometh."—Vide verses 28—29.

† A comparison of Psalm 118. with Matthew 21. 43—45 will show that Christ connects the righteous nation of Israel with the "stone"—the stone kingdom of Daniel, and Isaiah (27. 6) testifies to Israel as being the fruitbearing, witnessing, missionary nation.

extended in the near future, notwithstanding, the declared object of this Country, that its interference in the affairs of Turkey is solely prompted by a desire to promote the welfare of the downtrodden subjects of the Sultan. The Great Powers, in spite of all our protestations to the contrary, still persist in believing that England has some selfish object in view for her own aggrandisement.

That this Country is really sincere in its declaration there can be no doubt, but circumstances over which England will virtually have no control, will, as explained later on, ultimately bring about unexpected developments, which will in the eyes of the European Nations, apparently give a flat contradiction, to the oft expressed declaration, that the nation is only animated with the desire to protect distressed and persecuted humanity.

It is probable that only those who study the political situation in the light of revealed prophecy, can anticipate with any degree of approximation, the results of the destruction of the Turkish Empire, but not the means, by which that object will be attained, when that inevitable conclusion is a realised fact in the very near future.

All present indications foreshadow that the

Probable Division of Turkey in Europe

will be amongst the surviving victorious Continental Powers. Constantinople may be, however, as has been lately pointed out by General Sir Arthur Cotton, ultimately destroyed by an earthquake, judging from passages in Isaiah 34. 1—15; and Ezekiel 35. 1—13; where the destruction of Bozrah, or

Mount Seir is mentioned as caused by a volcanic disturbance.

The Division of Turkey in Asia, etc.,
is predicted under circumstances which leave no room for doubt, who will come into possession of the Sultan's dominions in that part of the world.

They will all become British-Israel Territory.

If any one doubts this statement let them turn to the sure word of prophecy "whereunto ye do well that ye take heed as unto a lamp shining in a dark place."

God has declared unto our Forefather Abraham:

"To thy seed have I given this land, from the river of Egypt unto the great river, the river Euphrates."

The River of Egypt in this promise is undoubtedly the Nile, as affirmed by the latest authority on Scripture Geography.* The Wady el Arish is only a winter torrent.

A glance at the annexed Map will at once bring home to the mind of the reader, that nearly all the Countries included in these Boundaries are part of the Ottoman Empire.

It is remarkable that the "seed of Abraham" has always been in the possession of some portion of the Promised Land, in its successive occupation by the Children of Israel, the Arabs, and the Turks, the respective descendants of Jacob, Ishmael and Esau, all of the seed of Abraham; and now shortly to revert again once and for all

---

* The S.P.C.K. Bible Atlas, edited by Sir George Grove, points out the distinction between the Hebrew word *nahar*, "river" used here, and the *nachal*, "brook" of Egypt, used of the Wady el Arish. *Ozonian.*

time to the elect seed, the Children of Israel in the direct line of Abraham, Isaac, and Jacob.

"For Esau is the end of the world, and Jacob is the beginning of it that followeth." (2 Esdras 6. 9.)

Few people seem to be aware how many countries are included in the Promised Land, so prone are they to confine the inheritance of the Chosen People to that narrow strip of territory on the Coast of the Mediterranean, alternately designated Palestine, or the Holy Land.

In examining the Map in detail, it will be observed that,

Egypt,

though nominally Turkish, is practically a British possession by virtue of our occupation. It is true that England is under an obligation to evacuate Egypt, so soon as in the opinion of our Government, it is able to stand by itself. Notwithstanding that the condition of Egypt has admittedly made a vast improvement under our able administration, much still remains to be done. There is only too much reason to fear that if the Land of the Pharoahs was handed back again to the corrupt government of the Turkish Pashas, that the work of years would be speedily undone.

However much they may talk, it is fairly evident that neither a Liberal or Conservative Government, has ever practically shown the slightest disposition to evacuate Egypt, even to please our jealous neighbors the French.

It is generally recognised that the Expedition into the

Soudan

has indefinitely postponed our evacuation of the Khedive's dominions.

Judging from the speeches of our excellent Prime Minister, Lord Salisbury, England has three objects to attain in sending the present Expedition to reconquer the Soudan.

1. This Country undertook at the time of putting down the rebellion of Arabi Pasha, and taking over the Administration of the Country ; to leave Egypt in a better condition than we found it : measured by the Nile, the Khedive's territory was twice the length it now is—this has to be restored.

2. It is a supreme effort on the part of England to put down once and for all, the horrible oppression and cruelty of the Mahdi. Slatin Pasha computes that nearly eighty per cent. of the population of the Soudan have been destroyed by cruelty, disease, or famine ; whilst vast tracts of fertile land have become little better than a howling wilderness.

3. It is hoped by the success of our arms, not only to restore the Egyptian Frontier to its original boundaries, but by so doing, to thereby make more effective our claim to control the Upper Waters of the Nile, as the paramount Power in Egypt. The Expedition has already been successful in recapturing the Province of Dongola, and doubtless will eventually complete its work by occupying Khartoum.

It will probably surprise many who have not given the subject a thought, to know that

Uganda

is included in the Promised Land. It is now a

British possession. Already our Missionaries, as evidenced by the Reports of the Church Missionary Society, are exercising a wonderful influence for good amongst the native population, and Mr. Johnston, the British Commissioner for Central Africa, in his last Report observes: "I regard the development of this country as little short of marvellous."

A Railway, too, has lately been sanctioned and is in course of construction at the expense of England, which will not only bring very great, and still more rapid, increase of prosperity to that part of Africa, but will also, probably, sooner or later, join the projected line from Cairo to Khartoum.

Further it will be observed that our Protectorate of

British East Africa,

rounds off England's possessions to the Indian Ocean. Thus apparently unheeded by the Nation at large, has about one fourth of the Promised Land unconsciously passed into the possession, occupation, or sphere of influence, of its destined Inheritors.*

Thus is the seed of Jacob supplanting that of Esau.†

What a commentary on the prophecy of Ezekiel (chap. 36. 8).

"But ye, O mountains of Israel, ye shall shoot forth your branches, and yield your fruit to my people Israel; *for they are at hand to come.*

Turning up round by

---

* It is true that Egypt and the Soudan are nominally Turco-Egyptian territory, but for all practical purposes, it is virtually under the control of England alone.

† See colored portions of the Map.

The Red Sea,

it will be noticed that our Troops—"your valiant men shall be clothed in scarlet"—are quartered at Aden, and also at Suakin, etc.

In referring to

Arabia,

it is interesting to recall the declaration of Jeremiah (chap. 49. 21—22) anent the downfall of Turkey:

"The earth trembleth at the noise of their fall; there is a cry, the noise whereof is heard in the Red Sea.

"Behold he shall come up and fly as the eagle, and spread out his wings against Bozrah: and the heart of the mighty men of Edom at that day shall be as the heart of a woman in her pangs."

A glance at the Map will illustrate the force of this declaration, for it will be observed that

Mecca and Medina

are there placed. What Jerusalem is to the Christians, these Towns are to the Mohammedan people—the Holy Places of the followers of Mohamet.

The consternation of the Mohammedan people when they see the Sultan, the titular head of their religion, deposed, and his dynasty overthrown by the Admiral of British-Israel, as the outcome of the advance of the Fleet, when it metaphorically "spreads out its wings—or sails—against Bozrah," or Constantinople, by the order of the Government of British-Israel, may be better imagined than described. The earth will then indeed "tremble at the noise of their fall."

It is as well to remember, however, that Her Majesty the Queen rules over quite as many, if not more, Mohammedans than the Sultan of Turkey, and it will be the interest, no less than the duty, of our Government to see, that the Holy Places of our Mohammedan fellow-subjects, are properly guarded and their religion respected.

The following incident, as related by a Correspondent of *The Standard* in *The Scotsman* of April 11th, 1896, on the subject of " The Arabs and the Sultan," is full of import at the present time. It is related as follows by one who was present :—

" During the annual pilgrimage lately, whilst a small and select party from Syria and Constantinople were visiting the shrines at Mecca, the Sheik ul Islam, ushering them into the Most Holy Place, and standing before the Beit-Ullah, or Tabernacle of God, prayed aloud that the scourge of Turkey might be quickly removed from them, even if it were by the English taking over the guardianship of Mecca and Medina. The pilgrims were thunderstruck, but kept silence ; but the tale is now slowly being passed along, and probably losing nothing in the telling—another weapon winging its way towards fated Yildiz. Nothing can be added which would lend additional force to this picture of the feelings of the latter-days Arabs towards their Ottoman Suzerain."

That this prayer will be realised ere long who can doubt ?

It has been pointed out in the Daily Newspapers that England could not allow any other Great Power of Europe to hold Arabia when it fell from the grasp of the Turk, as it is necessary to this Country in order to protect the left flank of our route to India.

The Arabs have yielded but the barest outline of allegiance to the Sultan of Turkey ; but no doubt, under the wise and firm administration of the British Government, these turbulent subjects of the Ottoman Empire will be reduced to order, and pilgrimages will be undertaken by " the faithful " to Mecca, with as little fear of molestation, as those of Christians of the present day to Jerusalem.

That enterprising traveller, Mr. Theodore Bent, in his paper on the "Exploration of the Frankincense Country," contributed to *The Geographical Journal*, writes as follows :—" Probably no country in the habitable world is at present so little known as Arabia. Arab fanaticism, waterless wastes, piracy and brigandage, have all combined to exclude Europeans, and now that we know so much of the history of Greece, Egypt, Palestine, and other Oriental countries from monumental records, Arabia is about the only place left that will afford us new and startling discoveries in the study of primitive mankind." As to

Muskat, the Capital of Oman,

Mr. Bent describes it as "bearing the same relation to the Persian Gulf that Aden does to the Red Sea, and *it is now practically British*, as far as the environments of the town are concerned, and the Sultan occupies much the same position as the native independent princes do in India. If it were not for British protection, and the presence of our gunboat in the harbour, Sultan Feysul, the present ruler, would have long ago succumbed to the attacks of the chiefs from the interior." " I may here emphatically state." continues Mr. Bent, "that the southern coast of Arabia has *absolutely nothing to do with Turkey*, and from Muskat to Aden there is not a single tribe paying tribute or having any communication with the Ottoman Porte."

A reference to *Whittaker* will also show that the independent Tribes on the south and east coasts of

Arabia, are in treaty relations with the Government of India.

The British Political Resident at Bushire, is the recognised arbiter in the quarrels of the Tribes on the east coast. The peace of the Gulf is maintained by the British Flag.

Abyssinia, or Cush.

The Italians, in vain pursuit of a colonial policy, have been desirous of establishing their authority not only over Erythrea, but also the whole of Abyssinia: the disastrous defeat at Adowa has brought home to the nation the folly and expense of such an enterprise. The energies of the Italian Government are now concentrated on the means how best to withdraw from the country without further loss of *prestige*. Such are the providential means of preventing the Italians creating a further obstacle, to the recovery later on, of the Chosen People's Birthright. Abyssinia, therefore, seems likely to preserve its independence for the time being.

It is interesting to note that there are a number of Jews in Abyssinia, where they bear the name of Falashas, or 'immigrants'; and that Zephaniah (3. 10) mentions this country as one of the districts from whence British-Israel "shall bring my suppliants, even the daughter of my dispersed for an offering."

Armenia.

The abominable and unmentionable atrocities committed on the unfortunate inhabitants, by the Kurds and Turkish Soldiers, at the command or connivance of the Sultan, have attracted the attention of the whole civilised world, and have stirred up a feeling of mingled horror and indignation not only in this country but also in America.

It may be remembered that numerous Schools have been built and maintained in different parts of Armenia, by the American Missions, and these buildings have all been more or less destroyed by the Turkish Authorities during the late massacres of the unfortunate Armenian Christians, who, to their everlasting honor be it said, preferred in many instances, to sacrifice their lives to their faith.

At one time it seemed quite probable that forcible means would have been taken by the Great Powers to put a summary stop to such diabolical proceedings: indeed, if telegraphic dispatches in the Daily Newspapers be correct, there can be no doubt that Lord Salisbury, when the occurrences took place, was anxious, nay willing, to send the Fleet up the Dardanelles, and depose the Sultan, etc., with a view to instituting a better and more humane administration at Constantinople. Austria, however, withdrew at the last moment, fearing that such extreme measures might precipitate a worse evil, namely, a general European war. The political situation in this particular respect is, for the time being, comparatively peaceful, and it is difficult, if not impossible, to forecast what particular incident may bring about such an event as our occupation of Armenia, but should we ultimately do so, we shall thereby gain control of the Upper Waters of the Euphrates, in the same way as by our occupation of Egypt, we now claim and exercise our right to control the Upper Waters of the Nile.

That the future possession of Armenia is inferentially assured to this country, is extremely probable for three prophetic reasons.

1. This Province of Turkey is within the boundaries of the Promised Land.

2. The declaration of the Prophet Esdras, in the following passage :

" Now when they shall begin to come,

" The Highest shall stay the springs of the stream again, that they may go through : therefore sawest thou the multitude with peace.

"*But those that be left behind of thy people are they that are found within my borders.*

" Now when he destroyeth the multitude of the nations that are gathered together, he shall defend his people that remain.

" And then shall he show them great wonders." (2 Esdras 13. 47—50.)

3. The Prophet Isaiah declares (27. 13) :

And it shall come to pass in that day, that a great trumpet shall be blown : and they shall come which were ready to perish in the land of Assyria."

Some part of Israel therefore, will be in that district of Armenia, as well as elsewhere, at the time of their entry into the promised inheritance.

The announcement of Isaiah is also of import, in view of the belief that is gaining ground among many Christians of the present day, that a certain portion of

These perishing Armenians are Rifts and Remnants of the Ten-Tribed House of Israel, left behind by the main body on their journey into Europe from the former scene of their captivity in the Cities of the Medes, towards their destined home in the British Isles of the Sea. These unfortunate Armenians hold many customs and traditions which point to their Israelitish origin. If this belief is correct, then recent events are full of significance, in view of the sympathetic feeling between this country and Armenia : it proves once more the truth of the old saying, that " blood is thicker than water."

Palestine.

The Holy Land *par excellence*, as distinguished from the Promised Land, of which it is only a very small part, but associated with memories dear to every Jew as well as Christian—to the Jews, as the land of their Forefathers and their future Inheritance—whilst to the Christian, it is hallowed by the footsteps, and the scene of the life of the Redeemer of Israel, and the Saviour of the World. How happy then the lot of the conscious British-Israelite, who delights in the privilege of sharing the memories and the hopes of *both* Jews and Christians ? Another answer to the *Cui Bono* question.

The cry of the inhabitants of the Holy Land is the same there, as elsewhere in the Sultan's dominions, " When are the English coming ? " As an instance of this expectation, which is testified to by many travellers through Palestine, the following incident is related by the late Commander Cameron in his interesting book—*Our Future Highway.*

" The old Zaptieh who had been given us as a guide at Homs said :

"In days gone by there were Sultans who cared for the people, and made bridges and roads; now there is no Sultan, and he who is called Sultan does not care for his people, and eats their money, and makes no roads or bridges; but when the English come that will be all changed, and we shall again have roads and bridges, Inshallah!"

Mention is also made of the following incident in connection with his visit to Baalbek.

"The poorer classes, indeed, have an idea, which was retailed to us as a compliment, that the English, whom they regard as the first of mechanics, lived here in some forgotten time, and that the ruins are the signs of their dominion."

It is also significant that the following telegraphic despatch from Béirût, recently appeared in *The Standard*:

"Recent events in Constantinople have caused considerable anxiety to the impressionable Syrian Christians. Though events have hitherto hardly seemed to justify this anxiety, the British Government has ordered the cruiser stationed off Alexandretta to come and show the British ensign from time to time at Béirût, in order to allay the fears of the Christian population."

It is recorded in the New Testament that,

"Jerusalem shall be trodden down of the Gentiles until the time of the Gentiles be fulfilled."

Also, "And the holy city shall they tread under foot forty and two months." This is the same period of time expressed in different terms, and is universally admitted to represent forty-two months of thirty days each, equivalent, on the "year-day" computation, to 1260 years. From the rise of the Mohammedan power over Jerusalem in A.D. 637, this time would run out in 1897; but Professor

Dimbleby has shown, in his wonderful, unique, and interesting Pamphlet, entitled "*The New Era at Hand*,"* that, owing to alterations by Parliament in our mode of reckoning, this period will not expire until the Spring of 1898.

Mr. Dimbleby states, " that the Bible is the only book in the world whose dates, years and months, are strictly those of astronomical motion, and to obtain their practical value, it is best to use them straight forward from Creation, or according to the A.M. Era, as they are accompanied by eclipses and transits, of which those of Venus and Mercury are better than eclipses that occur every year."

" But, we cannot do this with our Roman years used in England, because they are not natural years. We thus see, that by using these Roman years with Biblical history, the connection of Scripture time with scientific or astronomical time is lost, and all the prophecies and events are obscured."

Daniel's Dates

Are worked out in a marvellously clear and comprehensive manner by Mr. Dimbleby who observes, " that the great prophecies of Scripture have a most remarkable feature by ending as they began, that is to say they end on the same year as the cycle, same month, same date of the month, and same day of the week, on which they began. Yea, more, for they end when the eclipses are of the same character."

It is a matter for infinite regret, that owing to

* Can be obtained of the Book Society, 28, Paternoster Row, E.C., Price 3d.

POLITICS AND PROPHECY.

the Author's inability to distinguish between the prophetical passages which only apply to Israel and not to Judah, that some of his inferences are so misleading that they may ultimately descredit an otherwise apparently perfect method of chronological computation.

"The times of the Gentiles," end when Turkey ceases to "tread down the Holy Places," as Mr. Dimbleby correctly anticipates, but this event is not synonymous with "the Fulness of the Gentiles" which expression alone refers to the filling up of the Gentile nations, by the Lo-Ammi outcast House of Israel as explained in the preceding pages.

With this explanation, and accepting Mr. Dimbleby's dates, but not all his applications of *future* events to them, the following arranged extract from *The New Era at Hand*, may prove of interest.

"The Times of the Gentiles began with the four universal Empires called 'beasts,' in A.M. $3376\frac{1}{2}$, when Babylon became mistress of the world. Those of the Jews, thirty years later, with the captivity in $3406\frac{1}{2}$.

Thus :—

Gentile Times.	Jewish Times.
$3376\frac{1}{2}$	$3406\frac{1}{2}$
2520	2520

A.M. $5896\frac{1}{2}$, our A.D. $1898\frac{1}{4}$ A.M. $5926\frac{1}{2}$, our $1928\frac{1}{4}$

The periods of the four 'beasts' are as follows :—

$3376\frac{1}{2}$ first beast arose and the Gentile times of 2520 years began.

90 years, Babylon, the 1st beast continued—the lion.

200 years, Medo-Persians, the 2nd beast continued—the bear.

304 years, Grecians, the 3rd beast continued—the leopard.

$3970\frac{1}{2}$

3970½ Jerusalem became tributary to Rome, when the empire was proclaimed.
  666 years, Rome, the 4th beast continued to hold Jerusalem. Then ended the first 1260 years.
4636½ Saracens, the Mohammedan power, entered Jerusalem.
1260 years, the Mohammedan power—"the little horn" is to continue. See Daniel vii. 25.
5896½ will be 1898¼, A.D., at Easter, the 2520 years of Gentile times end. Turkey will cease to tread down the Holy Places.
   30 years more make 1260 into the 1290 of Dan. xii. 11.

5926½ our 1928¼, A.D., the 2520 years of Jewish times end.
   45 years more make 1290 into 1335 of Dan. xii. 12.

5971½ our 1973¼, A.D., refers to some further development of the Everlasting Kingdom of God on Earth.

Up to the year 4636½, all the above is history as well as Scripture, and in 1898¼ we shall reach another point."

Mr. Dimbleby notes: "that some Christians think that the words in Dan. vii. 22 'and judgment was given to the saints,'* indicate that they will take part in the condemnation of 'the little horn' before he is removed on the completion of his 1260 years."

The coming Occupation of Palestine by England.

What events will bring this about time alone will show.

All parts of the Sultan's dominions are reported as being in a seething state of discontent and rebellion. Crete is struggling for independence, and in Arabia, Palestine, and Asia Minor it is well known that the inhabitants are in a similar state of restlessness. The Troops of the Sultan are reported as throwing down their arms on account of their pay being a long time in arrear; the "Young Turkish Party" in Constantinople and

* But, "Saints" is a term alone applicable to Israel.

other parts of the Empire are agitating for the institution of reforms; but all is in vain, Edomite Turkey is steadily going to her doom.

When the dreaded, but none the less anticipated war breaks out, and all the European Powers except "isolated England" are involved in a war of mutual extermination; it is conceivable that public feeling will again be roused to put a stop to the bloodshed that it is anticipated will occur by the internicine strife amongst the various races included in the Ottoman Dominions, on the break up of that Empire.

England by thus putting a summary stop to further slaughter, may in this manner—as in Egypt —unwittingly place under her Protectorate all the countries included between the Euphrates and the Nile—the Land of Promise.

That the various races inhabiting these Territories will welcome the just and firm rule of the British Empire, there is not the slightest reason to doubt, and thus in spite of all present expressed intentions to the contrary, may the determination of this country be overruled and her destiny unconsciously fulfilled.

The Significance of England possessing the Holy Places of Jerusalem will not be generally recognised.

Many earnest Christians who now imagine that with the expulsion of the Turks from the Holy Land "the times of the Gentiles" will have come to an end, will, unless they are speedily able to realise the Israelitish origin of the British people, instead of regarding them as they now do as Gentiles, be much perplexed at the apparent non-fulfilment of Scripture, when Palestine becomes a British instead of, as they expect, a Jewish State or Settlement. Such a disappointment may naturally give rise to the thought in many minds, " Since the fathers fell asleep all things continue as they were." Scoffers will deride, and many whose faith is weak may fall away from a belief in the Scriptures.

What an argument that constitutes for the acceptance of British Israel Truth.

The Return of the Chosen People to the Land

will then be made easy, but it will only be a preparatory, not a final movement. *Prophecy, be it remembered, has a progressive, as well as a complete fulfilment.*

With Palestine and the Promised Land practically included in the Colonial Possessions of Great Britain, there will ensue a scene of political and religious excitement such as the world has never witnessed before. Business and religious sentiment combined, will bring about a tremendous rush for this favoured country, for favoured it will undoubtedly be by both God and man, when it comes under the rule of the British Crown, as experience has shown elsewhere all over the world.

Already vast numbers of Jews, driven out by persecution from other European countries, have come over to these Islands and America, * whilst

---

* What a commentary this is on the invocation, *not blessing* of Moses, contained in Deuteronomy 33. 7 :

" Hear, Lord, the voice of Judah. and bring him in unto his people : Let his hands be sufficient for him, and thou shalt be an help against his adversaries."

some are settling down in the Holy Land. But this movement amongst the Children of Israel, as the outcome of Judenhätze, or Jew baiting in Russia, &c., is not the glorious return of the Houses of Israel and Judah to their inheritance, which is predicted to take place under very different circumstances and conditions, at the close of this Dispensation.

Among Oriental Jews the belief is widely held, that the

Construction of Railways in Palestine

is a sign of the near approach of the Restoration.

This expectation is persumably based on the declarations of the Prophet Nahum (2. 3—4):

"The chariots flash with fire of steel *in the day of his preparation*—railway carriages emitting sparks by the wheels skidding.

"And the fir trees are shaken terribly." the "sleepers"—which are made of fir trees—as the trains rush over them.

"The chariots rage in the streets, they jostle one against another in the broad ways: the appearance of them is like torches, they run like the lightenings"—as the trains rush through the broad junctions, at night-time.

The Prophet Baruch (chap. 5. 5—7) not only testifies in the same manner, but gives details of the construction of the Railways. As the Apocrypha is so little read, it may be interesting to give the passage in full.

"Arise O Jerusalem, and stand on high, and look about towards the east, and behold thy children gathered from the west unto the east, by the word of the Holy One, rejoicing in the remembrance of God.

"For they departed from thee on foot, and were led away of their enemies: but God bringeth them unto thee exalted with glory, as children of the kingdom.

"For God hath appointed that every high hill, and banks of long continuance, shall be cast down [cuttings] and valleys filled up [embankments] to make even the ground, that Israel may go safely in the glory of God."

The Jews go back to Palestine in British Ships.

Isaiah (chap. 18), speaking in figurative language of the sails of our ships, says:

"Ah, the land shadowing with wings, which is beyond the rivers of Ethiopia."

"That sendeth ambassadors by the sea, even in vessels of papyrus, upon the waters." . . .

"In that time shall a present be brought unto the Lord of hosts *of* a people . . . *from* a people . . . to the place of the name of the Lord of hosts, the mount Zion."

Again (Isaiah 66. 20):

"And they shall bring all your brethren out of all the nations for an offering unto the Lord, upon horses and in chariots, and in litters, and upon mules, and upon SWIFT BEASTS,[*] to my

---

[*] An extract quoted by "*The Banner of Israel*," mentions that the Hebrew word translated "swift beasts" in the English Version is "kirkaroth," and occurs only once in all the Bible. The roots of the word are found in 2 Samuel 6. 14, where it is applied to the swaying dance of David, and in the common Hebrew word for furnace. Hence the derived meaning, "a swaying furnace." The English rendering

holy mountain Jerusalem."

Further, Isaiah says (11. 10—16):

"And it shall come to pass in that day, that the Lord shall set His hand again the second time to recover the remnant of His people, which shall remain, from Assyria, and from Egypt, and from Pathros, and from Cush, and from Elam, and from Shinar, and from Hamath, and from the islands of the sea."

"And he shall set up an ensign for the nations, and shall assemble the outcasts of Israel, and gather together the dispersed of Judah from the four corners of the earth. . . ."

"They shall put forth their hand upon Edom and Moab: and the children of Ammon shall obey them."

The Jews will go back in Unbelief

under the Mosaic Law, as according to Zechariah, they will refuse to believe in Christ until His Second Advent, "when they shall look upon him whom they have pierced, and mourn for him as one mourneth for an only son."

Anticipating an Objection that there will not be room in Palestine

to hold all the people, it must be borne in mind that the return will only be in a representative form so far as the British section of the Children of Israel are concerned, because Jeremiah (chap. 3. 14), predicts with reference to the "backsliding" House

---

"dromedary" is unjustifiable, as the accepted equivalent of which in Isaiah 60. 6, is a totally different word. It most accurately describes the furnaces of our modern Steamships, riding on the waves of the sea, and in a lesser degree Railway Engines (Nahum 2. 3, 4), already referred to.

of Israel, as distinguished from the "rebellious" House of Judah, that "I will take you one of a city and two of a family, and I will bring you to Zion."

The Settlement of the Twelve Tribes in the Holy Land

will ultimately be according to the details contained in Ezekiel (chapters 47 and 48); it will also permit, "The strangers that sojourn among you, which shall beget children among you, they shall be unto you as the homeborn among the children of Israel: they shall have inheritance with you among the tribes of Israel."

But, in order to obtain this privilege, they will have to conform to the religious customs of the children of Israel, judged by the following passage in Isaiah 56. 3--8:

"Neither let the stranger, that hath joined himself to the Lord, speak, saying, the Lord will surely separate me from his people."

"Also the strangers, that join themselves to the Lord, to minister unto him, and to love the name of the Lord, to be his servants, everyone that keepeth the sabbath from profaning it, and holdeth fast by my covenant;

"Even them will I bring to my holy mountain, and make them joyful in my house of prayer; their burnt offerings and their sacrifices shall be accepted upon my altar: for mine house shall be called a house of prayer for all peoples."

"The Lord God which gathereth the outcasts of Israel saith, Yet will I gather others to him besides his own that are gathered."

No such restrictions are mentioned in connection

with the wider territory included within the Boundaries of the Promised Land, therefore, presumably they do not exist.

The Temple will be built in great magnificence according to the designs contained in the Book of Ezekiel.

Palestine will become a most Prosperous Country.

The Prophet Amos declares,

" Behold, the days come, saith the Lord, that the plowman shall overtake the reaper, and the treader of grapes him that soweth seed ; and the mountains shall drop sweet wine, and all the hills shall melt.

" And I will bring again the captivity of my people Israel, and they shall build the waste cities,* and inhabit them : and they shall plant vineyards, and drink the wine thereof; they shall make gardens, and eat the fruit of them."

" And I will plant them upon their land, and they shall be no more plucked up out of their land which I have given them, saith the Lord thy God" (Chap. 9. 13—15).

And of Jerusalem, the following message is put into the mouth of British-Israel, to declare unto their Brethren the Jews :

" Comfort ye, comfort ye my people, saith your God.

" Speak ye comfortably to Jerusalem, and cry unto her, that her warfare is accomplished, that her iniquity is pardoned : that she hath received of the Lord's hand double for all her sins."

" O thou that tellest good tidings to Jerusalem,

* See Appendix, page 163.

lift up thy voice with strength; lift it up, be not afraid; say unto the cities of Judah, behold your God" (Isaiah 40. 1—9).

"There shall yet old men and old women dwell in the streets of Jerusalem, every man with his staff in his hand for very age.

"And the streets of the city shall be full of boys and girls playing in the streets thereof" (Zechariah 1. 4—5.)

The Future Political Union of the Jews, and British People under one King.

"In that day will I raise up the tabernacle of David that is fallen, and close up the breaches thereof; and I will raise up his ruins, and I will build it as in the days of old."

"That they may possess the remnant of Edom, and all the nations which are called by my name, saith the Lord that doeth this" (Amos 9. 11—12).

"And thine house, and thy kingdom shall be made sure for ever before thee; thy throne shall be established for ever" (2 Samuel 7. 16).

Dr. Grant says: "To make this passage, 'I will raise up his ruins, and I will build *it as in the days of old*,' imply as some contend, 'the conversion of heathen,' who never had anthing to do with David, or his tabernacle either, is manifestly absurd."

According to the chronological computation contained in "*The New Era at Hand*," it is remarkable that the promise as above, conveyed to David by the Prophet Nathan, "was given in the year 2963½, and its fulfilment is connected with the completion of the seven times of punishment inflicted on the House of Judah."

"The end of the Jewish Times of 2520 years from the captivity of Babylon in 3406 is 5926¼ or our 1928¼.

"The prophecy of the Everlasting Kingdom reaches this final date, and is exactly half way from Creation.

"Now 5926 is equivalent to our A.D. 1928, and completes the 1290 days of Daniel* (chap 12. 11.)"

It therefore seems a fair inference that this restoration of "the tabernacle of David that is fallen," will then take place.

The future Invasion of Palestine by Russia.
takes place as predicted by Ezekiel in chap. 38.

Russia is accompanied on that occasion by,

"Persia, Cush, and Phut with them; all of them with shield and helmet. Gomer, and all his hordes; the house of Togarmah, in the uttermost parts of the north, and all his hordes; even many peoples with thee."

"In the latter years thou shalt come into the land that is brought back from the sword, that is gathered out of many peoples, upon the mountains of Israel, which have been a continual waste: but it is brought forth out of the peoples, and they shall dwell securely, all of them."

* Although the 1290 years of Daniel xii. 11, are necessarily included in the Jewish seven times, or 2520 years, yet the 1335 years are not. They form part of the period having its commencement with the Gentile times in 3376. Indeed, it is clear that both periods are mentioned to notify the completion of two events, first, the end of the Jewish times, and secondly, the completion of the 6000 years of the age of the world, thus: $3376 + 1290 + 1335 = 6001$. But observe, 6001 is the first day of that year. The age of the world is computed in the same way as the age of man. No man is 30 years old till he comes to the first day of his 31st year. Hence the words: "*cometh to* the 1335 days."

"And thou shalt ascend, thou shalt come like a storm, thou shalt be like a cloud to cover the land, thou and all thy hordes, and many peoples with thee.

"Thus saith the Lord God: It shall come to pass in that day, that things shall come into thy mind, and thou shall devise an evil device:

"And thou shalt say, I will go up to the land of unwalled villages; I will go to them that are at quiet, that dwell securely, all of them dwelling without walls, and having neither bars nor gates:

"To take the spoil and to take the prey; to turn thine hand against the waste places that are now inhabited, and against the people that are gathered out of the nations, which have gotten cattle and goods, that dwell in the middle of the earth."

"Sheba and Dedan, and the merchants of Tarshish, with all the young lions thereof, shall say unto thee, Art thou come to take the spoil? hast thou assembled thy company to take the prey? to carry away silver and gold, to take away cattle and goods, to take great spoil?"

The quotation is long, but its importance is its own justification, for it is even,

The Time of Jacob's Trouble,
but he shall be saved *out of* it,"—not *from* it.

This is the time, when according to Jeremiah (30. 6), "every man is with his hands on his loins, as a woman in travail, and all faces turned into paleness."

Think what all this means. It means that after this great European War, all the lands now included in the Boundaries of the Promised Land, having been brought under the Protectorate of the British

Empire, will thereby in scriptural language constitute,

England as King of the South, whilst Russia
will become King of the North, or of Assyria,* by virtue of their occupying the geographical and territorial positions, assigned to these kings in prophecy. The present European Nations, stirred up by a spirit of jealousy that is already rampant amongst them, will, in "the last days," combine under the leadership of Russia, in order to revenge themselves on England for her apparent selfishness in taking advantage of their coming life and death struggle, to aggrandise herself at their expense, although involuntarily, of their anticipated share of "the sick man's inheritance." Thus towards the close of the next century, may be expected a confederacy of nations, with Russia at their head, for a life and death struggle, with the British Empire for the mastery of the world.

Professor Birks in his work *Two Later Visions of Daniel*, says: speaking of

Gog's Confederacy.

"Egypt alone seems too feeble to undertake any serious resistance to a confederacy so vast and mighty. . . .

"That the same power which holds the vast southern empire of India may then also have possession of Egypt, and from thence push against the inroads of its northern adversary, it would be

---

* This argument is very ably and briefly worked out, by Dr. Aldersmith in his pamphlet, "*Coming Events in the East, etc.*"

rash to expect with confidence, but the conjecture is not unreasonable. The course of events and the necessities of commerce appear more and more to be grouping together India, Egypt, and Britain...

"When, therefore, all the continent shall be gathered under one head, as King of the North, it seems not improbable that the maritime empire of Britain may be the rival power, and that its acquisition of Egypt will give to it the prophetic character of the King of the South. The great leader of the North will overthrow and pass on to the South, to crush the power that has assailed him. The description answers exactly to the words of Ezekiel, where he predicts the march of Gog against the land of Israel"—This is the time of

The Great Tribulation.

With reference to which Daniel predicts:

" And at the time of the end shall the king of the south contend with him : and the king of the north shall come against him like a whirlwind, with chariots, and with horsemen, and with many ships ; and he shall enter into the countries, and shall overthrow and pass through.

" He shall enter also into the glorious land, and many countries shall be overthrown : but these shall be delivered out of his hand, Edom, and Moab, and the chief of the children of Ammon.

" He shall stretch forth his hand also upon the countries : and the land of Egypt shall not escape.

" But he shall have power over the treasures of gold and of silver, and over all the precious things of Egypt: and the Libyans and the Ethiopians shall be at his steps.

" But tidings out of the east and out of the north shall trouble him : and he shall go forth with great fury to destroy and utterly to make away many.

" And he shall plant the tents of his palace between the sea and the glorious holy mountain ; yet he shall come to his end, and none shall help him " (chapter 11. 40—46.)

" And when they have made an end of breaking in pieces the power of the holy people, all these things shall be finished." (Daniel 12. 7).

These lengthy quotations from

Ezekiel and Daniel, throw a wonderful light on the present drift of political events.

Looking at the Map, after reading the foregoing passages, the whole situation is clearly brought before the mind of the reader.

Russia, in company with Persia, already under her influence: Abyssinia, or Cush, to whom Russia has been making advances for some years past: Gomer—Gomer-man or German man,* and all his hordes made up of the Confederate States : the house of Togarmah and all his hordes, the Asiatic Khanates or Tartar Tribes, who are so fond of riding on horses which are famous for their powers of endurance : Libya, or that part of Africa, probably coming under the influence of France, the ally of Russia at the present time : " even many peoples,"—" these have one mind, and they give their power and authority unto the beast for one hour."—*i.e.*, a short space of time—will on this

* This is a debatable point.

momentous occasion come up against England who will have for Allies, the Arabians (Sheba), Dedan and the "Merchants of Tarshish," and all the "young lions" or Colonies, and India.

How ominously significant the jealous feeling and attitude of nearly all the Powers towards this Country at the present time, and does it not afford an evidence of what may be expected at "that day," when the united Armies and Fleets of the Russian Confederacy of Gog will be so nearly successful in attaining the object in view, under the leadership of the Prince of Rosh, Meschech and Tubal, now, and then, represented by the Czar of of Russia, Moscow, and Tobolsk!

"And I will call for a sword against him unto all my mountains, saith the Lord God: every man's sword shall be against his brother.

"And I will plead against him with pestilence and with blood: and I will rain upon him, and upon his hordes, and upon the many peoples that are with him an overflowing shower, and great hailstones, fire and brimstone.

"Behold, I am against thee, O Gog, prince of Rosh, Meschech and Tubal.

"Thou shall fall upon the open field:

"And they that dwell in the cities of Israel shall go forth, and shall make fires of the weapons and burn them . . . and they shall make fires of

* The '*Merchants* of Tarshish' of these 'last days', are unquestionably represented by the Merchants, &c., of the old East India Company, and their present successors, the Government of India; this is evident by the nature of that country's merchandise as detailed in 1 Kings, 10. 22. For the same reason, the '*Ships* of Tarshish,' refer to those of the British Isles, *vide* Ezekiel 27. 12, *but both Merchants and Ships, are represented by, or belong to, one and the same people, viz., British-Israel, of the East and the West!*

them seven years.

"So that they shall take no wood out of the field, neither cut down any out of the forests; for they shall make fires of the weapons: . . .

"And it shall come to pass in that day, that I will give unto Gog a place for burial in Israel, the valley of them that pass through on the east of the sea . . . . and they shall call it the valley of Hamon-Gog."

"And seven months shall the House of Israel be burying of them, that they may cleanse the land" (Ezekiel, chapters 38 and 39).

"And at that time shall Michael stand up, the great prince which standeth for the children of thy people: and there shall be a time of trouble, such as never was since there was a nation even to that same time: and at that time thy people shall be delivered, everyone that shall be written in the book.

"And many of them that sleep in the dust of the earth shall awake, some to everlasting life and some to everlasting contempt.

"And, the teachers that be wise shall shine as the brightness of the firmament: and they that turn many to righteousness as the stars for ever and ever" (Dan. 12. 1—3).

Thus shall the enemies of God's Chosen People perish.

From Zechariah it is evident that *about* the time of this tribulation

The Second Advent of our Lord

takes place.

"And his feet shall stand in that day upon the

mount of Olives, which is before Jerusalem on the east."

"And I will pour upon the house of David, and upon the inhabitants of Jerusalem, the spirit of grace and of supplication; and they shall look unto him whom they have pierced: and they shall mourn for him, as one mourneth for his only son, and shall be in bitterness for him, as one that is in bitterness for his first-born."

S. Matthew thus records the words of our Lord:

"But *immediately after* the tribulation of those days, the sun shall be darkened and the moon shall not give her light, and the stars shall fall from heaven, and the powers of heaven shall be shaken:

"And then shall appear the sign of the Son of man in heaven: and then shall all the tribes of the earth mourn, and they shall see the Son of man coming on the clouds of heaven with power and great glory.

"And he shall send forth his angels with a great sound of a trumpet, and they shall gather together his elect from the four winds, from one end of heaven to the other." (S. Matthew 24 29—36).

"But of that day and hour knoweth no one, not even the angels of heaven, neither the Son, but the Father only." *

"But watch ye at every season, making every supplication, that ye may prevail to escape all these things that shall come to pass, and to stand before the

* Mr. Dimbleby remarks on this passage: "We do not know the day, or hour. More than this we do not know the month; nay, we know not the year. But we well understand the period, because in Dan. 7. 13, it is definitely stated in words of great sublimity."

Son of man." (S. Luke 21. 36).

Jerusalem to become the Central City of the Earth.

At the time of Christ's appearing on the Mount of Olives, Zechariah declares :

" And the Mount of Olives shall cleave in the midst thereof towards the east and towards the west, and there shall be a very great valley ; and half of the mountain shall remove towards the north and half of it towards the south.

" And ye shall flee by the valley of my mountains, for the valley of the mountains shall reach unto Azal ! yea, ye shall flee, like as ye fled from before the earthquake in the days of Uzziah King of Judah : and the Lord my God shall come, and all the holy ones with thee."

The late Major J. Scott-Phillips, in his interesting Pamphlet, *The Re-Settlement of All Israel in Syria and Arabia*, shows that the effect of this earthquake will be to, " make the Mediterranean come rushing in. For Surveyors have shown us that the level of the Dead Sea is 1,312 feet below the Mediterranean, and if we draw a line to represent the major axis of the Mount of Olives and divide the line by a perpendicular thereto, we shall find that on the east, the division immediately reaches the Dead Sea, and on the west, if prolonged so as to indicate the course of a very great valley, it will reach unto Ascalon, whereof the *sc* changed into *z* produces Azalon, and cutting off the termination *on* will bring the valley even unto Azal on the coast of the Mediterranean. An earthquake valley being opened, the waters of the Great Sea, falling eight times the depth of the Niagara into the Dead Sea, will speedily cause its waters to rise ; and while a mighty whirlpool will be created in the vast basin of the Dead Sea, its rising waters will be quietly permeating the drift sands of four thousand years which now conceal the southern bed of the Jordan.

"Yes, as surely as the waters of the Mediterranean shall enter the Dead Sea at an angle—and admirably prepared as the geographical construction of the surrounding mountains is to produce a grand gyration—so surely will that gyration of commingled water rise from a hollow swirl to a mighty overpowering swell.

"And when at length the waters stand upon an heap, and the sustaining power of gyration ceases to uphold, the mass of water falls and separates and strikes against the surrounding mountain sides : 'and now let him that is in the valley flee unto the mountains' to escape the rising waters.

"'Let the sea roar, and the fulness thereof ;
 Let the floods clap their hands ;
 Let the hills sing for joy together ;
 Before the Lord, for he cometh to judge the
  earth :
 He shall judge the world with righteousness,
 And the people with equity' (Psalm 98. 7—9).

"'And God will make a way in the wilderness and
  and rivers in the desert.'

"We have spoken of an assumed earthquake shock, as by the Prophet Zechariah, dividing the Holy Land from west to east ; but if at the instant swelling overflow, a second shock should act from north to south, cleaving afresh the old bed of the

Jordan, and elevating the floor of the Dead Sea, then the tumultuous waters, finding no other outlet, will rush down the Jordan's bed, cleansing it in a moment.

"The Dead Sea rising above its desolate shores, will overflow by the Valley of Edom, completing the Straits of Azal into the long Red Sea, by the Gulf of Akabah. Thus Jerusalem become the central city of the earth, will stand upon the highway for all nations. And the riches of the East and of the West will then find their great Emporium; and religion reigning above commerce in those coming happy days, will fill that long-despised down-trodden city with the glory of the earth; and

God will Extend Peace to Jerusalem
like a river, and the glory of the Gentiles like a flowing stream.

"The Dead Sea shall receive the living waters of the ocean; and thus shall be formed *the* great pool of Jerusalem—the harbour for the commerce of the world."

The same event which brings about this change, may also see the fulfilment of Isaiah's prediction of

The Destruction of the Tongue of the Red Sea.

"And the Lord shall utterly destroy the tongue of the Egyptian Sea; and with his scorching wind shall he shake his hand over the River, and shall smite it into seven streams, and cause men to march over dry shod." (Chapter 11. 15).

Major Scott-Phillips observes on this passage:

"The rush of waters—possibly aided by a North

wind—because Scripture says, "And with his mighty wind shall he shake his hand over the river of Egypt."—will sweep down the re-opened bed of the Jordan; and as the Gulf of Akaba is straight, and its sides steep, the sands will not rest there, but in the quiet back eddy behind the roots of Sinai—there among the narrows and islands will the mass of sand be deposited; and when once the swell of the Red Sea is bounded thus, speedily waters will fail from the tongue of the Egyptian Sea *—the Sea of Suez; and as by the maps of the Surveyors of the Red Sea, the Bay of Cosseir is opposite to the Gulf of Akaba, and since, as by the maps of the savants who accompanied the first Napoleon to Egypt, as well as by the maps of the Society of Useful Knowledge, there exists an old river bed, stretching from Cossier to the Nile, the rush of waters, swollen as aforesaid and pressed on by a mighty north wind, will push up that ancient river bed—plunge into the Valley of the Nile, with heaps of mud and sand, and in their refluent course drag after them the waters of the Nile, thus " beating off from the channel of the river " into the Red Sea."

Zechariah declares :

"And it shall come to pass in that day, that living waters shall go out from Jerusalem: half of them towards the eastern sea, and half of them towards the western sea; in summer and in winter shall it be.

"And the land shall be turned as the Arabah, from Geba to Rimmon south of Jerusalem, and

* ("Query: What then will become of the Suez Canal.")

she shall be lifted up, and shall dwell in her place." (Chapter 14. 8—10).

The Origin of Different Nations,

now gradually emerging from obscurity will be made known, for Isaiah declares that then God:

" Will destroy in this mountain the face of the covering that is cast over all peoples, and the veil that is spread over all the nations.

" He hath swallowed up death for ever; and the Lord God will wipe away tears from off all faces: and the reproach of his people shall he take away from off all the earth: for the Lord hath spoken it." (Chapter 25. 7).

Oxonian, in his Introduction to *Russia Japhet, p. 2*, says:

" A reference to the original of the first part of this passage shews at once that 'all peoples' denotes not all individuals but all clans, communities, or peoples—being literally *all the peoples*. So too the closing words are, all the wider *ethnic* units, *all the nations*. 'The covering cast over' them is *the hiding that hides* them, for such is the signification of the Hebrew root."

The Millenium

then ensues, during which Christ in His humanity, reigns with His saints for a thousand years.

"And the Lord God shall give unto him the throne of his father David:

And he shall reign over the house of Jacob for ever: and of his kingdom there shall be no end." (S. Luke 1. 32—33).

"And he shall judge between the nations, and shall reprove many peoples: and they shall beat their swords into plow-shares, and their spears into pruning-hooks: nation shall not lift up sword against nation, neither shall they learn war any more" (Isaiah 2. 4).

"And it shall come to pass, that everyone that is left of all the nations which came against Jerusalem shall go up from year to year to worship the King, the Lord of Hosts, and to keep the feast of tabernacles.

"And it shall be, that whoso of all the families of the earth goeth not up unto Jerusalem to worship the King, the Lord of Hosts, upon them there shall be no rain.

"And if the family of Egypt go not up, and come not, neither shall it be upon them; there shall be the plague, wherewith the Lord will smite the nations that go not up to keep the feast of tabernacles.

"This shall be the punishment of Egypt, and the punishment of all the nations that go not up to keep the feast of tabernacles.

"In that day shall there be upon the bells of horses, HOLY UNTO THE LORD; and the pots in the Lord's house shall be like the bowls before the altar.

"Yea, every pot in Jerusalem and in Judah shall be holy unto the Lord of hosts: and all they that sacrifice shall come and take them, and seethe therein: and in that day there shall be no more a trafficker in the house of the Lord of Hosts." (Zechariah 23. 16—21).

"Then Cometh the End."

"When he shall deliver up the kingdom to God

even the Father: when he shall have abolished all rule and all authority and power.

"For he must reign, till he hath put all his enemies under his feet.

"The last enemy that shall be abolished is death.

"For, He put all things in subjection under his feet. But when he saith, All things are put in subjection, it is evident that he is excepted, who did subject all things unto him.

"And when all things have been subjected unto him, then shall the Son also himself be subjected to him that did subject all things unto him, that God may be all in all." (1 Cor. 15. 24—28).

SO MOTE IT BE.

POSTSCRIPT.

The Author desires to acknowledge his indebtedness,—unintentionally omitted in the Preface—to Philo-Israel (E. W. Bird, Esq.), the able honorary Editor of *The Banner of Israel*, to whose publications he is primarily indebted for knowledge of British-Israel Truth. The introductory arguments in this Pamphlet, are in a large measure derived from a study of the works of the Leader of the Anglo-Israel movement.

Thanks are also due, and are heartily accorded to Oxonian, for the many valuable suggestions he has given the Writer, in the compilation of this Pamphlet.

Much useful information has also been gleaned, by a continuous study for many years past, of *The Banner of Israel*, and *The Covenant People*, the official weekly and monthly Press organs of the British-Israel Association; to which publications the energetic Secretary of the Society, the Rev. F. Aston, Vicar of Bushbury, Wolverhampton, has contributed many original and instructive articles. To the numerous Authors of various articles in these publications, the Writer expresses his sincere thanks for varied information and instruction he has derived from a perusal of their writings on this most interesting subject.

In conclusion, the Writer hopes that any who may be convinced by a perusal of this Pamphlet, of the truth of the argument therein contained, will enrol themselves as Members of the British-Israel Association, and take an active part in proclaiming the truth, of this, the greatest discovery of the age.

H. H. P.

APPENDIX.

"The Waste Cities" of Isaiah.

Literal *versus* Spiritual Israel.

"The Waste Cities" of Isaiah.

The following extracts, taken from "*The Giant Cities of Bashan*," by the Rev. J. L. Porter, A.M., (1866), will give a faint idea of what these wonderful " Waste Cities " are like at the present time.

" Bashan was regarded by the poet-prophets of Israel as almost an earthly paradise.

". . . . We enter the domains of Bedawin, whose law is the sword, and whose right is might. Our further progress was liable to be disputed at any moment. The attacks of the Bedawin, when made, are sudden and impetuous. . . .

" So it is always now in this unfortunate land, where the Ishmaelite roams free.

" The ancient cities and even the villages of Western Palestine have been almost annihilated with the exception of Jerusalem, Hebron, and two or three others . . . . The state of Bashan is totally different: it is literally crowded with towns and large villages; and though the vast majority of them are deserted, *they are not ruined*. *

" Many of the houses in the ancient cities of Bashan are perfect, as if only finished yesterday.

" Let not my readers think that I am transcribing a passage from the 'Arabian Nights.' I am relating sober facts; I am simply telling what I have seen.

" But how," you ask me, " can we account for the preservation of ordinary dwellings in a land of ruins ? . . . . The reply is easy enough. The houses of Bashan are not ordinary houses, their

* The italics throughout the quotations, are in the original.

walls are from five to eight feet thick, built of large squared blocks of basalt; the roofs are formed of slabs of the same material, hewn like planks, and reaching from wall to wall; the very doors and window-shutters are of stone, hung upon pivots projecting above and below.

"Some of these ancient cities have from two to five hundred houses still perfect but no man to dwell in them.

In the time of St. Paul "there were no fewer than *thirty-three* bishoprics in the single ecclesiastical province of Arabia. The Christians are now nearly all gone, but their Churches are there still . . . . noble structures some of them are, with marble colonnades and stately porticos.

"There was something to me inexpressibly mournful in passing from the silent street into the silent church.

"Not less than thirty of the threescore cities of Argob were in view at one time; . . . . their black houses and ruins half-concealed by the black rocks amid which they are built, and their massive towers rising up here and there like the "keeps" of old Norman fortresses.

"Scrambling through, or rather over, a ruinous gateway we entered the city of Bathanyeh. A wide street lay before us, the pavement perfect, the houses on each side standing, streets and lanes branching off to the right and left. There was something inexpressibly mournful in riding along that silent street, and looking in through half-open doors to one and another of those desolate houses. . . . . . One of the houses in which I resided for a time might almost be termed a palace . . . . Greek inscriptions on the principal buildings proved that they existed at the commencement of our era . . . . the whole town has probably been deserted for at least a thousand years."

Speaking of Kenath, Mr. Taylor says:—"the general aspect of the city is very striking—temples, palaces, churches, theatres, and massive buildings, whose original use we cannot tell, are grouped together in picturesque confusion."

With reference to the general aspect of the land, the Author states:

"The fields are waste, the roads deserted, the cities abandoned, the houses without inhabitants, the sanctuaries desecrated, the vineyards, orchards, and groves destroyed.

"In the vale immediately to the south of Salcah . . . . I counted *fourteen* towns, all of them so far as I could see with my telescope, habitable like Salcah, but *entirely deserted!* From this one spot I saw *upwards of thirty* deserted towns! (Jer. 48. 15-24).

"The walled cities of Bashan, with their ponderous gates of stone, are there now as they were when the Israelites invaded the land, . . . There are the roads once thronged by the teeming population; there are the fields they enclosed and cultivated; there are the terraces they built up; there are the vineyards and orchards they planted; all alike desolate, not poetically or ideally, but literally "without man, and without inhabitant, and without beast." . . . It was a sad and solemn scene.

"Remounting our horses we rode along the silent streets and passed out of the deserted gates into the desolate country. . . . and took a last look at Salcah. . . . Everthing seemed so complete, so habitable, so lifelike, that once and again I looked and examined as the question rose in my mind, *"Can* this city be totally deserted?" Yes, it was so:—" without man and without beast."

"Leaving Kerioth . . . we passed several small villages perched like fortresses on projecting cliffs, and we saw other larger ones in the distance; they are all deserted.

"The whole history of the country for four thousand years, from the Rephaim down to the Osmanlis is written there (*i.e.*, in Bashan). The massive dwellings show the simple style and ponderous workmanship of *Giant* Architects. *Jewish (sic)* masonry and names; *Greek* inscriptions and temples; *Roman* roads; *Christian* churches; *Saracenic* mosques; *Turkish* desolations,—all, all are there; and all alike are illustrations of the accuracy and confirmations of the truth of the BIBLE."

*   *   *   *

It will probably surprise many of our Brethen of America when they are informed that Bashan was allotted to their Forefathers—the half-tribe of Manasseh, in common with the tribes of Reuben and Gad—in the Mosaic Age, and also to be told that when the Re-Settlement of All Israel takes place according to the lines prophetically indicated by the Prophet Ezekiel, some portion of this country will again be theirs!

Literal *versus* Spiritual Israel.

The Right Rev. J. C. Ryle, Lord Bishop of Liverpool, in "*Coming Events and Present Duties*," says—" I think we have made great mistakes, and it is high time that we should confess it.

"I warn you that unless you interpret the prophetical portion of the Old Testament in the simple, literal meaning of its words, you will find it no easy matter to carry on an argument with an unconverted Jew . . . . Will you dare to tell him that Zion, Jerusalem, Jacob, Judah, Ephraim, Israel, do not mean what they seem to mean, but mean the Church of Christ. . . . .

"I believe it is high time for the Church of Christ to awake out of its sleep about Old Testament prophecy. From the time of the Old Fathers Jerome and Origen down to the present day men have gone on in *a pernicious habit of 'spiritualising' the words of the prophets until their true meaning has been well nigh buried* . . . . .

It is high time for Christians to interpret unfulfilled prophecy by the light of prophecy already fulfilled. The curses on the Jews were brought to pass literally; so also will be the blessings. The scattering was literal; so also will be the gathering. The pulling down of Zion was literal; so also will be the building up. The rejection of Israel was literal: so also will be the restoration.

"*It is high time to cease from explaining Old Testament prophecies in a way not warranted by the New Testament.* What right have we to say that the words Judah, Zion, Israel and Jerusalem ever means anything "but literal Judah, literal Zion, literal Israel and literal Jerusalem? What precedent shall we find in the New Testament? Hardly any, if, indeed, any at all.

"I can only discover three senses in which the word Israel is used:

"First, it is one of the names of Jacob.

"Second, a name given to the Ten Tribes which separated from Judah and Benjamin and became a distinct Kingdom, often called Israel in contradistinction to the Kingdom of Judah.

"Third, the name given to the whole Jewish *(sic)*, or Twelve-Tribed nation. . . . .

"Have promises been held out to Israel? Men have been told continually that they are addressed to Gentile Saints.

"Have glorious things been described as laid up in store for Israel? Men have been incessantly told that they describe the victories and triumphs of the Gospel in Christian Churches. . . .

"Against that system I have long protested, and I hope I shall always protest as long as I live. . . . .

"*Where, in the whole New Testament, shall we find any plain authority for applying the word Israel to any one but the Nation Israel? I can find none* . . . .

"In reading the words which God addressed to His Ancient People, *never lose sight of the primary sense of the text.*" *

* The Italics in the above quotation are not in the original.

This important declaration entirely accords with the views of Anglo-Israelites, as the following extract from

"British-Israel Truth" *

plainly shows.

"We cannot admit the arguments of our spiritualising opponents who declare, . . . that Israel's promises *only* are to be spiritually undertood, as meant for the Christian Church in all ages, nations, creeds and climes. Those who make the statements have resting on them the burden of proof, that such special dealing with the case of Israel *only* is justifiable ; and must explain why the promises regarding Christ and the Jews were all literally fulfilled in time past, and all are being literally accomplished at the present hour.

"The spiritualisers of the prophecies have not done this yet, and till they do, we must be content to regard their pleas as outside the case with which we have to deal in the present work." *vide* Page 17.

In connection with the foregoing quotations, it is gratifying to record the following introductory

Remarks by the Right Rev. Bishop Beckles,

(late of Sierra Leone), when presiding over "a well attended and influential audience at the Assembly Rooms, St. Leonards," † on 4th February, 1897, to hear a Lecture by the Writer, on the Anglo-Israel Theory and the Turkish Problem, as dealt with in the preceding pages. His Lordship observed that he had "read up the subject some

---

* A Handbook for Enquirers published by the Authority of The British-Israel Association.

† Vide "*The Hastings and St. Leonards News.*"

years ago, and again recently, and he felt convinced of its importance. If the Anglo-Saxon race were not the lost House of Israel where were they? He regretted the Clergy did not give the matter the study it deserved, especially as so many in their congregations were deeply interested in it."

May God grant that the apparent indifference towards this subject by " the Shepherds of Israel " may soon pass away.

ENGLISHMEN ISRAELITES.

Tabulation of Contents.*

A Great People	42
A Mighty Empire and a Company of Nations	41
A Multitudinous Race	43
Abrahamic Covenant, The	36
Africa	50
Anglo-Israelites	47
Anglo-Israelism, Interpretation not Doctrine	7
Appointed Place, The	44
Army and Navy, An Invincible	50
Assyria to the British Isles, From	12
Benjamin	24
Blessing to other Nations, A	53
Birthright Blessings	40
British Empire and Stone Kingdom Identical	78
Church, The	69
Church and State, The Union of	54
Clergy experience difficulty in accepting this Theory, The	101
Commentators and Theologians	100
Cui Bono	86
Dan	90
Different Names	27
Divine Protection, Under	48
Dominion of the Sea	48
Early History of the Children of Israel	7
Election and Predestination	97
Few Men read the Old Testament	100
Free Country, A	46
Foreign Loans	51
Gates of their Enemies	44

* This Index, whilst not adhering strictly to the head lines, is so arranged, as will best enable the reader in the Writer's opinion, to more readily find any particular argument or passage that may be required.

INDEX.

Hebrew Customs. Various other	56
Hints for Interpretation of the Scriptures	33
India	19
Jacob's Stone	65
Jew, Israelite, and Gentile	74
Jews, Missions to the	89
Kingdom of God, The	66
Language	33
Missionary People, The	48
Mosaic Covenant, The	36
National Church, The Service of our	83
New Testament proves Conversion of the Ten Tribes	75
Northern Kingdom of the House of Israel	10
Our Lord's Advent is proved by our Identity	89
Parables, The	80
Preface	3
Reason concerning the hope that is in you	90
Religion	35
Resumé of the Argument, A	82
Royal Family descended from David	56
Sabbath Keeping People, A	53
Saints, The term alone applicable to the Chosen People	96
Slavery and Oppression, Putting down	52
Suggestion to the Clergy, A	92
Trust in God	92
Warning and Explanation	97

TURKS EDOMITES.
POLITICS AND PROPHECY.

Tabulation of Contents.

Abyssinia or Cush	129
Arabia	126
Armenia	129
Armenians are rifts and remnants of the Ten Tribed House of Israel	131
Balaam, The Parable of..	108
British East Africa	125
Daniel's Dates	134
Egypt	123
End, Then cometh the	158
England and America alone	111
England as King of the South, Russia as King of the North, or Assyria	147
Esau is Edom	106
Ezekiel's Prophecy of Edom	107
Ezekiel and Daniel throw a wonderful light on the present drift of political events	149
Gangrene of Europe, The	118
General European War	119
Gog's Confederacy	147
Great Tribulation, The	148
Invasion of Palestine by Russia, The future..	145
Jacob's Trouble, The Time of	146
Jerusalem shall be trodden down of the Gentiles	133
Jerusalem is to become the Central City of the Earth	153
Jews go back in Unbelief	111
Jews go back to Palestine in British Ships	140
Mecca and Medina	126
Millenium, The	157
Muskat, the Capital of Oman	128
Obadiah, The Vision of ..	110
Objection that there will not be room in Palestine, Anticipating an	141

Obstacle, The Great	113
Occupation of Palestine by England, The Coming	136
Origin of the different Nations, The	157
Our Saviour's Prediction	119
Palestine	132
Palestine will become a most prosperous Country	143
Peace to Jerusalem	155
Political Union of the Jews and the British People under one King, The future	144
Politics and Prophecy	165
Railways in Palestine, The Construction of	139
Red Sea, The	126
Return of the Chosen People, The	138
Second Advent of our Lord, The	151
Settlement of the Twelve Tribes in the Holy Land, The	142
Soudan	124
The significance of England possessing the Holy Places will not be generally recognised	137
Tongue of the Red Sea, Destruction of the	155
Turks Edomites	105
Turkey in Asia, etc., Probable division of	122
Turkey in Europe, Probable division of	121
Uganda	124
What will bring about our joint interference in the affairs of Turkey	113
Woe betide the unspeakable Turk	117

INDEX TO APPENDIX.

Literal versus Spiritual Israel	167
Waste Cities of Isaiah	168

The British-Israel Association
1896.

PATRON:
THE RIGHT HONOURABLE THE EARL OF RADNOR.

VICE-PRESIDENTS:

Rev. ARCHIBALD ALISON, M.A.
Rev. ELIEZA BASSIN, B.A.
Rev. JAMES P. BRITTON, A.K.C.
Rev. A. E. BROWN.
Rev. R. LINGEN BURTON, M.A.
Rev. PHILIP CARLYON, M.A.
Rev. CHARLES HILL, M.A.
Rev. ROBT. HUNTER, M.A.
Rev. J. IDRISYN JONES.
Rev. E. J. KENNEDY.
Rev. JAMES McINTOSH, B.A.
Rev. JOHN McKAY.
Rev. JAMES MOUNTAIN.
Rev. A. PARKINSON, M.A.
Rev. MARK GUY PEARSE, M.A.
Rev. J. ANDERSON WATT, M.A.
Rev. E. J. WEMYSS-WHITTAKER.

Rev. J. WILD, D.D.
JOHN S. ANDERSON, ESQ.
LT.-GEN. M. DE LA POER BERESFORD
GENERAL GODBY.
GENRAL WM. HILL.
COL. THE HON. OLIVER LAMBART.
COLONEL W. H. LARKINS.
DR. ARTHUR PROWSE.
GENERAL RAINEY.
COLONEL SENIOR, I.S.C.
DR. HEYWOOD SMITH.
J. G. TAYLOR, ESQ.
COLONEL THOMPSON.
J. H. WELDON, ESQ.
COLONEL FINCH WHITE.
R. A. WHITTLAW, ESQ.
GENERAL MUSPRATT WILLIAMS.

COUNCIL:

DR. ALDERSMITH, F.R.C.S., Upper Wimpole Street, London.
Rev. MARCUS S. BERGMANN, Burdett Road, Bow.
E. W. BIRD, ESQ. ("Philo-Israel"), Tyndall's Park, Bristol *(Chairman)*.
DR. DYCE BROWN, M.A., Seymour Street, Portman Square, W.
FREDERICK C. DANVERS, ESQ., C.B., India Office, Whitehall, W.
RICHARD FOLKARD, ESQ., Bickley, Kent.
Rev. CHANCELLOR HANAN, D.D., The Rectory, Tipperary.
COL. HON. OLIVER LAMBERT, Southend-on-Sea.
CAPTAIN LOWE, Chepstow Villas, W.
LANDSEER MACKENZIE, ESQ., Bournemouth.
Rev. W. M. H. MILNER, M.A., ("Oxonian"), All Saints' Parsonage, Lockerbie, Scotland.
DOUGLAS A. ONSLOW, ESQ., J.P. *(Vice-Chairman.)*
H. H. PAIN, ESQ., Bromley, Kent.
J. HOPE-WALLACE, ESQ., J.P., Featherstone Castle, Northumberland.
J. CHAS. WARDROP, ESQ., Hans Road, Hans Place, S.W.

HON. TREASURER:
DR. ALDERSMITH, F.R.C.S., London.

HON. SECRETARIES:
REV. CHANCELLOR HANAN, D.D., Rector of Tipperary.
DOUGLAS A. ONSLOW, ESQ., J.P., 5, Upper Richmond Road, Putney, S.W.
(Vice-Chairman).

GENERAL SECRETARY:
REV. FREDERICK ASTON, Vicar of Bushbury, Wolverhampton.

EDITOR OF "THE BANNER OF ISRAEL:"
E. W. BIRD, ESQ. ("PHILO-ISRAEL"), Bristol.

EDITOR OF "THE COVENANT PEOPLE:"
REV. W. M. H. MILNER, M.A. ("Oxonian"), Lockerbie, Scotland.

BANKERS:
THE UNION BANK OF LONDON, Regent Street Branch.

The Association arranges for Lectures and Drawing-Room Meetings, and undertakes Public Meetings and Conferences in all parts of the Kingdom. It also undertakes to provide efficient Lecturers. The Rules of the Association can be obtained from the Secretary.

Extracts from Opinions of the Press

On the First Edition of this Work.

THE BANNER OF ISRAEL.

"......Mr. Pain......has in this volume gone over the whole ground of Our Identity, and in a short, terse argumentative fashion, told us the whole story, from the beginning to the end, of the origin, progress and future of the British Empire.......

Mr. Pain's merit is, that he focusses the whole into a page or two......

The work under review, no doubt, is a very valuable one, and should be of great service to all of us engaged in the propaganda of our glorious truth.

........It embraces every subject we all have at heart in connection with Our Identity........."

THE BIRMINGHAM GAZETTE.

"An irritating rigmarole of perverted prophecy and Scriptural quotation, endeavouring to prove that the British nation, with America, is identical with the House of Joseph (not Chamberlain), and that the destruction of Turkey will be brought about by their joint intervention. We wonder how the Sultan will bear up under this latest onslaught."

BROMLEY AND DISTRICT TIMES.

"The author endeavours to prove that the British Nation is identical with the House of Israel from the fact of being in possession of the Abrahamic blessings, so far as they have at present been fulfilled. Turkey is also connected with Edom, inasmuch as Edom is prophetically indicated as the Power in possession of the Holy Land, previous to the return of the chosen people. The concluding portion of the pamphlet goes to prove that on the foregoing assumptions, England alone will bring about the solution of the Turkish problem."

THE BULLIONIST.

" The author of this extraordinary book is so obviously in earnest that it would be almost cruel to treat the whole thing as a joke, as one is tempted to do at the first blush..... ..."

THE COVENANT PEOPLE.

"The author's........demonstration that "Englishmen" are "Israelites" is exhaustive, and his subsequent identification of the Ottoman Turks with Edom is most conclusive; while the specially engraved reduction of the large Map of the Promised Land, constructed for the author at Stanford's geographical establishment, shows the reader at a glance how far Jacob has already supplanted Esau in occupation of the Land.

Many a bit of good reading is to be culled from these pages; one of the very best being a most convincing answer, given item by item, to the old objection *Cui Bono?*........"

DUNDEE ADVERTISER.

" Starting with the belief that the British people are the descendants of the lost ten tribes of Israel, as distinguished from the House of Judah, Mr. Pain proceeds to forecast " the coming occupation of Palestine by England........

In Mr. Pain the subject has a capable and graphic exponent."

THE FINANCIAL TIMES.

"Mr. H. Herbert Pain, a well-known member of the Stock Exchange, has performed a great service to humanity by finding the Scriptural solution of the Turkish problem........and although his views may not be shared by Foreign Secretaries and Diplomatists, they cannot be ignored by thoughtful people........."

THE GLASGOW HERALD.

"This is a book in support of the extraordinary doctrine that the British nation is the lost ten tribes of Israel. It is written up to date, and not only finds the fulfilment of prophecy in events that are transpiring, but tells us with great confidence what is about to happen........."

The Jewish World.

" Mr. H. Herbert Pain, from whose pen we have recently published so many deeply interesting letters, has just written a little book in which he brings together a strong body of evidence in favor of the Anglo-Israel theory. We cannot say his arguments are convincing, but it must at least be admitted that they are not without some force."

The Jewish Chronicle.

"Anglo-Israelism is to solve the Armenian Question. This is the burden of Mr. H. Herbert Pain's volume.........."

The Queen.

"......Mr. H. Herbert Pain......gives all kinds of amazing reasons why the British people should call themselves Israelites, while the Jews should remain Jews."

The Rock.

"......Mr. Pain is certainly happy in his method, puts his arguments in the most telling form, and condenses a wonderful amount of matter really germane to his subject into the relatively small compass of a hundred narrow pages. If our readers have not made themselves acquainted with the subject.....we cannot recommend a better treatise than the one now before us. We cannot speak so favourably of the second section of the book. We have always understood that the posterity of Esau was hopelessly extinct...... Not that we should wish to assert dogmatically that the children of Esau are extinct......At the same time he writes interestingly. ......We hope we shall meet Mr. Pain again.

Reynolds.

"The author........seeks with much ingenious interpretation of the Bible to prove that the English are Hebrews, and, as such, have a special interest in safeguarding the holy places in Palestine............"

The Salisbury & Winchester Journal, & General Advertiser.

"......Some of Mr. Pain's speculations are ingenious, some are far-fetched........The book is readable, but as for pronouncing an opinion on its merits we must wait until the spring of 1898 to do that. At that time, it seems the Mohammedan power over Jerusalem will come to an end, and 'Turkey will cease to tread down the Holy Places.'"

THE SHEFFIELD TELEGRAPH.

"........The work is intended to convince Englishmen that they are the descendants of the lost Ten Tribes. One can fail to see why anyone should be anxious to persuade Englishmen that theirs is such a pedigree, and yet be free to acknowledge the ingenuity with which the author constructs his theory, and of the arguments with which he supports it.........The one thing upon which the book leaves no doubt is the author's sincerity and earnestness."

SOUTH AFRICA.

"If we were in a punning mood we might call this official-looking book a painful infliction. It has been made manifest to the author that the British nation and America constitute the House of Israel of the Old Testament prophets, and that the destruction of Turkey will be brought about by their joint intervention. It may be so; on the other hand, it may not."

THE WITNESS.

"........It would be impossible to give here even an outline of the evidences which Mr. Pain produces in proof of his contention. Our very name British, he says, is Hebrew, and he thinks he can discover many other marks in us of Hebrew origin."

WESTMINSTER REVIEW.

"We gather from this eccentric tract that Englishmen are Israelites (the lost Ten Tribes again), and that the Promised Land (see coloured map) is Egypt, the Soudan, and East Africa. From these premises it is easy to see how politics and prophecy meet in these latter days, and how the Stock Exchange and the Scripture are agreed as to our policy in the East."

List of some Books and Pamphlets, Etc., Recommended.*

British-Israel Truth.—5th Ed. (10,000)—A Handbook for Enquirers. Published under the authority of the British-Israel Association. Edited by Rev. CHANCELLOR HANAN and DR. H. ALDERSMITH. Price 1s., limp boards 1s. 6d.

A Message to the Church from the Nineteenth Century. By the Right Rev. BISHOP TITCOMB, D.D. Cloth Boards, price 1s. 6d.

The Fulness of the Nations; or the A B C of the Promises Given to the House of Israel, Considered in Relation to the Second Advent. By H. ALDERSMITH, M.B., F.R.C.S. Cloth, gilt, price 5s.

Israel: a Thesis. Treating of the Present-day Development of Ephraim's Birthright. By the Rev. CHANCELLOR HANAN, M.A., D.D. Cloth Boards, price 1s. 6d. (2nd edition.)

A Resume of the Scriptural Argument, Proving the Identity of the British Race with the Lost Ten Tribes. By PHILO-ISRAEL. Price 1d.; 6s. per 100.

Report of the Conference between the British-Israel Association and the Prophecy Investigation Society, at Exeter Hall, on May 2, 1895. 4d.

Russia Japhet; or, The Muscovite, The Cossack, and The Mongol; tracing in detail the Peoples named in Ezekiel xxxviii., xxxix. By "OXONIAN." Price 5s.

The Origin, Progress, and Establishment of the Kingdom of God in the World. By SURGEON-GENERAL GRANT, M.D. Cloth, gilt, Price 2s. 6d.; paper 1s.

Israel in the New Testament; or, Proofs of the National Conversion of the Ten Tribes to Christianity. A continuation of "The Covenants." By SURGEON-GENERAL GRANT, M.D. Price 4d.

The Evidence afforded by the "Speaker's Commentary" on British-Israel Truth. By Dr. ALDERSMITH, F.R.C.S. Price 1d.

Israel's Wanderings; or the Scuths, the Saxons, and the Kymry. By the Rev. "OXONIAN," M.A. Cloth, gilt, Price 3s. 6d.

The Covenant People; the Journal of the British-Israel Association, and a Monthly Expositor of the Prophecies concerning the two Houses of Israel and Judah. Price 6d.

Coming Events in the East; and the Return of the Jews to Palestine. By H. ALDERSMITH, M.B., F.R.C.S. Price 2d.

The Great Distinction between the "House of Judah" (the Jews) and the "House of Israel," in these 'Latter Days.' By DR. ALDERSMITH. Price 2d.

The Banner of Israel; a Weekly Journal advocating the Identity of the British Nation and Empire with the Lost Ten Tribes of Israel. Edited by PHILO-ISRAEL. Price 1d.

New Testament Truth; on the Anglo-Israel Controversy. By J. G. TAYLOR. Price 3d.

* These Books and Pamphlets can be obtained of Messrs. ROBT. BANKS AND SON, Racquet Court, Fleet Street, London.

"HEAVEN'S LIGHT OUR GUIDE."

THE BANNER OF ISRAEL.

A WEEKLY JOURNAL

Advocating the Identity of the British Nation and Empire with the Lost Ten Tribes of Israel.

Edited by PHILO-ISRAEL.

The Objects and Aims of the "Banner of Israel."

I.—To do our utmost to prove the absolute Identity of the British Race, as represented by the Empire, with the Lost Ten Tribes of Israel.

II.—We believe, and admit, there may be "rifts and remnants" of Israel and Manasseh still existing on the Continent of Europe, and that these are probably being gradually gathered into these Islands and the United States respectively in the providence of God. But Ephraim, and "the Tribes of Israel his fellows," we maintain, are, each and all, as to the bulk of these Tribes, already present in the British Empire.

III.—We believe, and shall endeavour to prove, that the British People are enjoying to-day exclusively, all those blessings which constitute the birthright of Joseph, that birthright which God's Word shows us He promised exclusively to "Ephraim and the Tribes of Israel his companions" (Ezek. xxxvii. 19, R.V.).

IV.—We shall argue thus, from the past that the British are "Lost Israel;" but we shall not venture to predict future events beyond that bare outline of such which God's Word plainly reveals.

V.—Our staff consists of about 30 writers, all of whom ably represent our views on the important subject, to elucidate which the "Banner of Israel" exists. We do not, of course, hold ourselves responsible for all their statements, or for all their views, as a certain latitude must of course be allowed for individual opinions. But generally their teachings will be found to be in conformity with ours, as above described.

VI.—Current events, as explained by Identity light, will, as heretofore, occupy a large portion of our space.

PUBLISHED EVERY WEDNESDAY: PRICE ONE PENNY.

In Monthly Parts, with occasionally a Coloured Map, Price 6d.

Sent post free in Weekly Numbers or Monthly Parts, to any part of the World for 7s. per annum, prepaid.

London: ROBERT BANKS & SON, Racquet Court, Fleet Street.
May be ordered of any Bookseller, and at Railway Bookstalls.

THE COVENANT PEOPLE
The Journal of the British-Israel Association.

A Monthly Expositor of the Prophecies concerning the Two Houses of Israel and Judah.

With which is incorporated

THE MESSENGER.

Edited by REV. W. M. H. MILNER, M.A. ("Oxonian.")

Author of "Israel's Wanderings," "Russia Japhet," &c., &c.

THE Resurrection of Israel in the English-speaking lands has found of late years a large number of believers, who naturally feel themselves to be closely united by the common possession of a great truth; nevertheless, so vast is the subject, and so many the side questions on which it touches, that it is not to be wondered at that much variety of view on minor points exists. To meet this variety of view, as far as may be consistent with discrimination as to what is likely to be of service to the cause of truth, is one of the principal objects of THE MESSENGER. The Editor, therefore, proposes to present for his reader's perusal any communications which may, from time to time, reach him bearing upon such points as these:—

Scriptural and Historical Proofs of the Migration of Israel into Britain. The Evidence of Language. Testimony of Irish Tradition. Imperial Federation. The National Position of the British Colonies. Progress of the British Race throughout the World. The Social and Political Life of the United States. Home Re-union. The Forward Policy of Russia. Contemporary Politics in France and Germany. Constantinople, Egypt, and Abyssinia. The Position, Power, and Persecution of the Jews. The Exploration of Palestine. The Future of Jerusalem and the Holy Land.

Published Monthly, price 6d. (post free 7d.), and in Yearly Volumes, price 6s.

May be ordered of any Bookseller.

R. FOLKARD & SON, 22, Devonshire Street, Queen Square, W.C.
R. BANKS & SON, Racquet Court, Fleet Street, E.C.

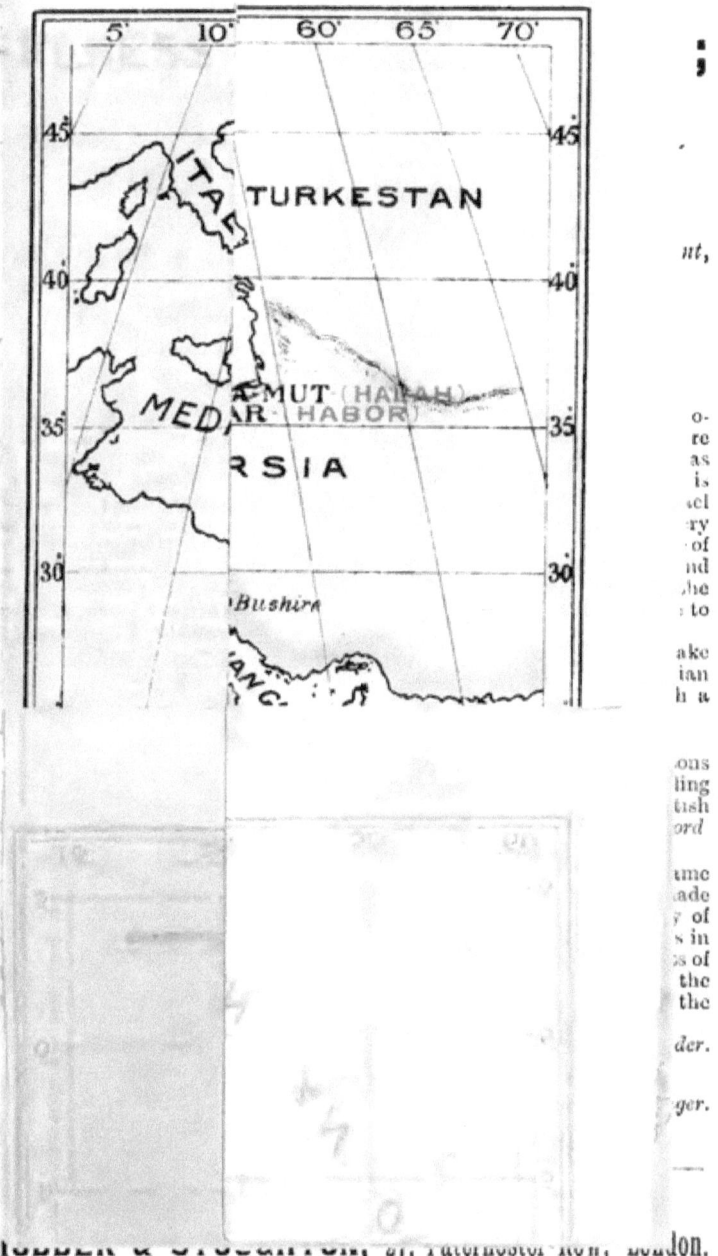

The Promised Land Gen 15.18.

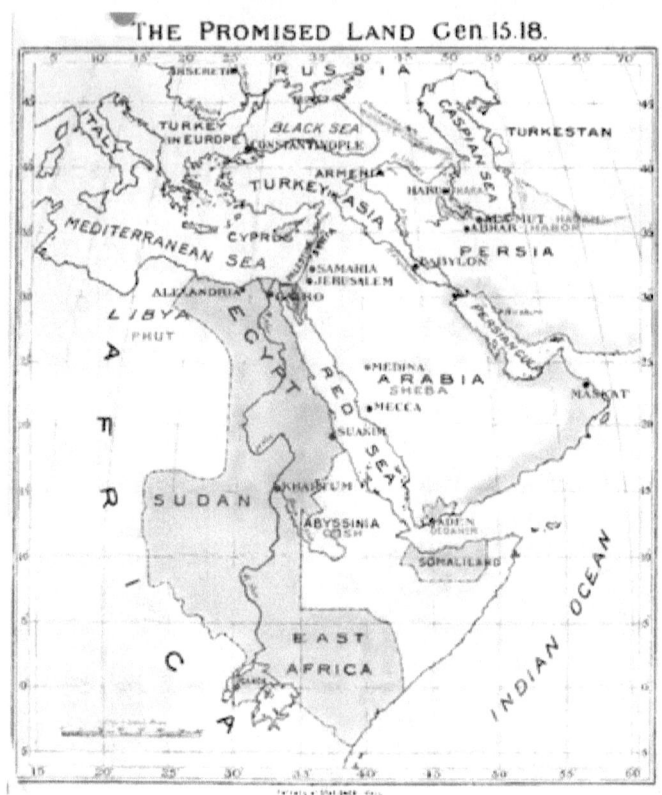

www.ingramcontent.com/pod-product-compliance
Lightning Source LLC
Chambersburg PA
CBHW020245170426

43202CB00008B/239